Tim's abiding passion is simply to know ⟨...⟩ being intimately connected to him. Tim ⟨...⟩ recollections weave vital discoveries throu⟨...⟩ this book without hesitation, whether you have trusted God for some time, or are just embarking on your journey of faith.

        **PAUL WAKELY** — Pastor

I am inspired, encouraged and challenged by what Tim has written in Mountainside Secrets. Going deeper with God is something that comes out of adoration not obligation. This book left me wanting to draw closer to Jesus, to spend time in the secret place.

    **DAN BLYTHE** — Global Youth Director, Alpha International

Jesus' primary mission on Earth was to reveal the heart of a loving Father. He is still doing that today. Mountainside Secrets is an invitation to live out a journey that is deeply connected with Jesus. Tim, in his honest and relatable style, helps you meet the Father afresh. Irreligious and illuminating, this book will help turn your time with Jesus into a lifestyle of ongoing secret-place encounters. It will change your view of God and inspire your prayer life. Get it, read it, and be changed by it!

    **JULIAN C. ADAMS** — International Prophetic Minister,
        author of Terra Nova and The Kiss of the Father.

I highly recommend you to read this book Tim has written about living a life devoted to God. It's not religiously presented but instead honest and vulnerable.

      **RAPHAELLA ELY** — (Found Youth)

Much can be said about this beautiful book, it's crafted writing, its curated stories and profound reflections but I must begin with words about the man behind its pages. I believe wholeheartedly that we must only write with words we've paid for and here is an author who has done just that. Writing about prayer, about the hidden life with Christ requires one to first live such an existence and pursue the practices that shape a life of intimacy with God. No one is more qualified to write such a book than my friend, my brother Timothy Rudge. Just as was said of his names sake in the New Testament, do not look down on this man because he is young. Tim writes with a wisdom that transcends his years, a passion that spills through his ink and a conviction born of suffering love, true dedication and prayer. I believe in generations to come, this book will rightfully sit alongside classic writings about our spiritual life. I'm so proud of you Tim.

**JOSHUA LUKE SMITH** — Pastor | Poet | Author

Timothy lives from a place of deep, personal intimacy with Christ. This short book gives a beautiful invitation to find your own place of soul's rest with God, and to linger in the kindness of His presence. My soul was stirred in reading it with a fresh sense of wonder for the beauty of these secret places.

**SARAH YARDLEY** — Mission Lead, Creation Fest

This is an important read, and one I'm sure will be beneficial for many.

**GUVNA B** — Rapper | Author

This book is a beautiful piece of poetic art. Tim's stories and insights ring with reality and pierce the culture of our day with timeless truths. The more you read the hungrier you get for more time with God.

**DAN REYNOLDS** — Pastor

# MOUNTAINSIDE SECRETS

A thoughtful guide for knowing God
in every day life

TIMOTHY RUDGE

Published by Orphan No More
Published 2022

Copyright © 2022

The right of Timothy Rudge to be identified as author of this work has been asserted by him in accordance with the Copyright, Designs and Patents Act 1988.

All rights reserved. No part of this publication may be reproduced, stored in a retrieval system, or transmitted in any form or by any means, electronic, mechanical, photocopying or otherwise, without the prior written permission of the publisher.

Unless otherwise stated, Scripture quotations are taken from THE HOLY BIBLE, NEW INTERNATIONAL VERSION®, NIV® Copyright © 1973, 1978, 1984, 2011 by Biblica, Inc.® Used by permission. All rights reserved worldwide.

Scripture quotations are taken from the Holy Bible, New Living Translation, copyright © 1996, 2004, 2015 by Tyndale House Foundation. Used by permission of Tyndale House Publishers, Inc., Carol Stream, Illinois 60188. All rights reserved.

Scripture quotations marked MSG are taken from THE MESSAGE, copyright © 1993, 2002, 2018 by Eugene H. Peterson. Used by permission of NavPress. All rights reserved. Represented by Tyndale House Publishers, Inc.

Scripture quotations marked TPT are from The Passion Translation®. Copyright © 2017, 2018, 2020 by Passion & Fire Ministries, Inc. Used by permission. All rights reserved. ThePassionTranslation.com.

The ESV® Bible (The Holy Bible, English Standard Version®). ESV® Text Edition: 2016. Copyright © 2001 by Crossway, a publishing ministry of Good News Publishers. The ESV® text has been reproduced in cooperation with and by permission of Good News Publishers. Unauthorized reproduction of this publication is prohibited. All rights reserved.

Scripture taken from the New King James Version®. Copyright © 1982 by Thomas Nelson. Used by permission. All rights reserved.

ISBN: 978-1-3999-3835-8

*British Library Cataloguing-in-Publication Data*

A catalogue record for this book is available from the British Library

# CONTENTS

Foreword     7
Introduction     9

**SECTION ONE: FINDING JESUS**     13
1. When the dancing stopped     15
2. What Billy taught me     29
3. Lightest load     41
4. Radical root     55

**SECTION TWO: BEING WITH JESUS**     65
5. Los Angeles     67
6. Body odour     75
7. His secret chapter     89
8. Cash-machine Christianity     97
9. Leave your camera in the car     105

**SECTION THREE: THE APPROACH**     115
10. Swimming through white water     117
11. Learning to live dethroned     125
12. Wrestling with God     131
13. Disarmed     137
14. Openings everywhere     141

**SECTION FOUR: PRACTICAL POINTERS**    149
15. A private pursuit    151
16. When and where    155
17. Psyche of a gardener    165
18. Bodybuilding mentality    175
19. Final words    183

Acknowledgements    191
Postscript    195
About the Author    199

# FOREWORD

Job made a remarkable statement when he wrote, "What is man, that You should...set Your heart on him, that You should visit him every morning?" (Job 7:17-18). Job was revealing the fact that God visits each one of us every morning.

He visits us because He's looking for friendship, for company, for companionship, for affection, for relationship. He just wants to be with us. And it all flows from a secret place relationship with Him.

If you're going to have a secret place relationship with Jesus in these current times, you're going to have to be *violent* (Matt 11:12). Because everything in our world is designed to squeeze out our secret place time with Jesus.

For starters, you're going to have to be violent with that device in your hand. You're going to have to be violent with distractions and demands.

Get out your sword, O mighty man of God, and cut back the distractions that want to squeeze out your secret time with God. Get out your sword, O mighty woman of God, and do violence to the things that want to rob you of an intimate relationship with Jesus.

This book is written as a guide to help you. As you make your way through this book, glean from Tim Rudge's years of experience, and find your own cadence with God in the secret place.

The next time God pays you a personal visit—that is, tomorrow morning—will He get your attention?

—**Bob Sorge**
Kansas City, USA
*August 31, 2022*

# INTRODUCTION

Sometimes when I hear preachers talk about 'pursuing God', I cringe. They use a different sort of language that seems to be totally removed from the real world and culture I'm living in. They remind me of Radagast the Brown in J. R. R. Tolkien's *The Hobbit*. He's a strange wizard with bird poo matted into his hair who spends his time talking to animals and riding a sleigh pulled by rabbits.

We are not supposed to stay in prayer rooms or attics. God doesn't want us to get weird and hairy, lost somewhere in the clouds. We were made for a purpose on this earth that involves work amongst real people.

Ephesians 2:10 says:

> For we are God's handiwork, created in Christ Jesus to do good works, which God prepared in advance for us to do.

However, from Thomas Merton to John Wesley, C. S. Lewis to Kathryn Kuhlman, our public life (what people see) has always been a direct result of what's done in private. Of course that can be said of many areas of life. No one would disagree that the championship-winning shots Michael Jordan achieved were ultimately a result of hours of balls in hoops no one saw. But it's the same in our walk with Jesus. A private pursuit of God seems to be an inescapable prerequisite for a lasting, life-filled relationship with God that goes out from us, affecting the world.

Some of you reading this will work in an office; or be missionaries caring for the poor; or farmers working 18-hour days to produce food; or kitchen fitters under pressure from your boss; or writers working to a deadline. You fill in the blank. But my prayer is that, if you cut us open, wherever we live and whatever we do as a 9–5, our blood would scream the same utter devotion to Christ, because in secret, we found God.

This is by no means a book with all the answers, but it's my own reflections, my own story to date of finding God and then re-finding him.

INTRODUCTION

## Note about questions and reflections at the end of chapters

I'm praying these musings would awaken you to your own story with God. I'm also praying as you read this book it will help you practically to begin finding God for yourself. I have included some reflections and questions at the end of some chapters; hopefully this will trigger, on a deeper and more personal level, your own application of the content. I know questions asked at the right time have often been critically helpful in my journey of discovery. I'm also aware that to some people they are a distraction. So there's no obligation to engage. Whether you doodle and annotate and enjoy questions or just want to read through without stopping either is fine, it's your book now!

# SECTION ONE
# Finding Jesus

# 1

# WHEN THE DANCING STOPPED

I am convinced the teenage years, especially from around 13 to 18, can be some of the most internally challenging and turbulent years of someone's life. They certainly were for me. By the time I was 16 I couldn't wait to leave school. If you had asked me at the time, I would have said I wanted to leave school because I was questioning whether what I was learning was relevant to life. But truthfully I think it was because I was just tired of feeling insecure. I remember frequently glazing over during algebra – largely because the maths block had big windows all across one side of the building facing out towards the school grounds. As soon as the classroom doors opened to let us in, I looked forward to lodging myself against the glass so I could stare through the windows towards the bottom of the playing fields and watch students skiving and making suspicious deals. Sometimes my eyes lingered even further beyond the green gates of the school and I indulged in daydreams of distant adventures on the farm with Billy at Ross-on-Wye where life was much more simple.

I remember clearly when we began studying for our final GCSE exams. It was as if an anxious mist descended on our year group. It flowed through the hallways, poisoning youthful conversations and creeping into classrooms where its weight started crushing students and teachers alike. Everyone seemed edgy. My travel and tourism teacher even broke down in tears during one lesson. These fast-approaching tests seemed like the defining moments of our very lives. In all honesty, I felt somewhat detached from the weighty expectation. I was set on leaving school despite my fairly decent predicted grades.

For the majority of my childhood all I wanted was to be a farmer like my dad. I visited a gigantic agricultural college in Gloucestershire called Hartpury the same year I was finishing school. When Dad and I arrived at the huge grounds, one of the lecturers showed us around the campus. He talked passionately about the Hartpury rugby team and how well they were doing in the local league. I immediate panicked, mental images flashing about being peer-pressured into joining the team; mainly because of a memory of being picked up and dump-tackled on the frozen ground one cold winter morning by a kid in my PE class called Jon.

After the rugby pitches the lecturer showed us some huge corrugated sheds with every type of machinery imaginable and a parlour where I would learn dairy farming. Afterwards we looked at the dorms. I stood in my potential future room and stared vacantly at the bed, full of fear. Dad was talking to the lecturer but it was as if they were on 'mute'. My adolescence became overwhelming and more apparent to me than ever before and the sudden, real prospect of leaving home turned my stomach into a nauseous knot. We didn't talk much on the drive home. I felt ashamed that I wasn't ready to leave home. Disappointed that I couldn't follow my dad's own love for farming.

I tried to move on quickly, exploring other options such as apprenticeships. If I wasn't going to do farming, I knew it would have to be some sort of trade, something practical and hands on. I had spent two weeks doing work experience with a carpenter, so I went to the school's careers office on one of my lunch breaks and was shown all the woodworking companies in the local area that I could write letters to and apply for any available jobs. Sitting in my smart, slightly dishevelled school uniform, surrounded by computers and coloured school tables, it felt as if I was peering into one of my make-believe worlds as I began visualising working in a workshop in the 'real' world. I sent off a whole pile of letters, still in disbelief that I was on the cusp of leaving school.

Only one company got back to me saying that they were interested in taking on an apprentice. I eagerly searched them on

Google and found out it was a joinery company that made all kinds of bespoke items for shops like Hotel Chocolat as well as pubs and restaurants all across the UK.
So at last I was escaping school and embracing a new adventure.

## The workshop
The first week in the workshop I felt incredible – I was earning a wage despite how minimal it was. I stared at my weekly notes as if I'd won the lottery. I watched, mesmerised, as Charlie made a unit that he said was going to be fitted in the new Cath Kidston store in Bath town centre. My mum shops in Cath Kidston and I told her proudly as soon as I got home. From the look on her face, Mum was assumed I was an integral part of its construction but I didn't bother correcting her.

Occasionally in the workshop I would slip into another daydream and imagine being skilled like the other guys and knowing I was capable of constructing anything I was tasked with by the boss. The reality was that most of the time I was making cups of tea for everyone and sensed I was a nuisance. I picked up a number of unwritten rules early on; for one, if I put my hands in my pockets I would get shouted at by someone in the workshop. Having your hands in your pockets meant you weren't busy enough – at least I think that's the logic. I quickly discovered the workshop truly was a different world to school. I started thinking enviously about my friends sitting in warm classrooms, chatting, carefree when they should be working on an assignment. After a while, I began questioning if I had made the right decision, leaving the familiar school buildings for this whole new environment I was struggling to get to grips with.

I felt guilty about every bit of grief I had given teachers. I realised they were extremely patient when compared to the guys supposed to be teaching me in the workshop. They swore aggressively at me when I delayed bringing them a tool or forgot to put sugar in their coffee.

One day I was ecstatic to be asked to do something actually related to woodwork, instead of cleaning toilets or walking the boss's dog. I proudly sanded a piece of wood for Chris using a large tool called a belt sander that could pull your arm out of its socket if you didn't brace it firmly enough. Sometimes I would go downstairs behind the machines where they stored wood to get a break from the onslaught of verbal abuse and the pressure to stay busy. Later on in the day Chris found me down there. Chris was older than the other guys, he was more gentle and didn't raise his voice, but he sounded very frustrated that day at the back of the workshop. He asked, 'Are you an idiot?'

I wasn't sure how to reply.

'You sanded that wood against the grain!' he exclaimed with a sigh and a face that spoke volumes about his lack of faith in me.

Later, when we passed on the stairway, he suggested seriously

I was never going to make it as a joiner and asked if I had considered doing something else.

Progressively I felt more rigid, like it was only a matter of time before I was going to make another mistake. I lost count of the numerous occasions I overheard the boss call me 'useless' to the other guys and slowly I started to believe it was true.

I cycled to the workshop every day in a high-vis waterproof jacket my parents had bought me for Christmas. I remember in the winter reluctantly leaving my house in the dark and arriving home in the dark, which started to make everything appear even worse. I would pedal home as quickly as I could, gripping the handlebars tightly, trying to avoid the puddles in the road as the rain dripped down through my helmet and onto my face. My mind regularly churned over what people had said that day, forming a case that I felt was beginning to mount up. I would question myself, 'What *is* wrong with me?' Then push harder on the pedals, trying to escape the scary feelings of self-hate storming my gates as if I was an overthrown castle.

When I got home from the workshop, I would put my bike in the passageway next to the back door of my house, take my raincoat off and hang it up, and often rush up the stairs to my room. I didn't let my parents into this internal crisis that was taking place – I didn't want them to worry or conclude that I was failing. They told their friends all the time how proud they were that I was learning a trade and doing something practical after school. I felt ashamed of the truth. That I was dying inside, I was not learning how to make woodwork for Cath Kidston but instead tidying up all day. But when I was in my room with the door securely shut I would cry and talk to God. God had always been real to me growing up. I remember when I was 8 having a conversation with him on the way to school as though he was physically walking next to me. But throughout secondary school I 'danced' with him a lot. What I mean is one moment I was pulling him close, and the next I was pushing him away and running into the arms of my friends, getting drunk at parties and trying to impress girls.

## Youth camp

Before I left school and started my apprenticeship I went to youth camps in the summer with my church. There would be thousands of young people who had driven from all kinds of places across the UK to camp together and discover more about Jesus. I had never seen so many Christians in one place. It seemed to rain every year during the camp even though it happened in the middle of the summer. You had to queue in thick mud surrounding the portaloos if you needed the toilet or wanted to brave a shower. Once, my friend Jacques accepted £2.50 to run, jump and dive head first into the mud whilst a random teenager filmed it on a flip phone.

In the evening, everyone excitedly came together in a huge marquee called the 'Big Top'. I met God during those meetings. Not because I got an acceptable academic explanation for his existence but because, in a mysterious, hard-to-explain way, he was there. In that tent surrounded by mud and tired eyes, the Jesus story collided with my own and suddenly my existence made a bit more sense.

At home, back in my dance with God, it became so easy to put him into the dark corners of my mind, whereas at those camps he became undeniably real and impossible to avoid. I remember one night, at the end of the meeting, the leaders prayed for people who wanted to receive 'God's love'. You had to stand up if you wanted to be prayed for. I stood up nervously without thinking it over too much. My heart was suddenly racing uncontrollably with so many of my friends looking up at me from where they were sitting on the floor, but I could feel something deep within me that longed to experience for myself this God of love I had so often heard about growing up. I sealed my eyes and everything became quiet within me. I could hear wailing and other strange noises coming from different places in the tent. I discovered later that God is partially spirit and therefore words and ordinary language rarely succeed in giving expression to his mysterious activity. But I will attempt to put into words how he moved in me that day. It was comparable to being wrapped in a warm weighted blanket, but somehow even my insides became warm, as if I was drinking a hot drink on an icy winter day. I started crying because my heart felt so heavy with this consuming warmth feeling, then I couldn't stop crying. I opened my eyes after what felt like a brief moment of time but it must have been a long while because almost everyone else had disappeared from the tent. I could hear shouting and music playing from the after-hours entertainment cafés. Only my youth leaders were left and they were staring at me like something serious had happened, as if I'd just woken up from a coma or had food on my face. I stood there motionless, taking it all in, looking around the tent, dazed as if I had just got back from another world, still with that sensation of comforting warmth bubbling inside me.

Eugene Peterson translates John 1:14 this way, which resonates deeply with my experience that evening:

> The Word became flesh and blood,
>   and moved into the neighborhood.
>
>                                           (MSG)

Certainly, that day in the tent surrounded by smelly feet, it felt as if Jesus had moved into *my* neighbourhood.

Those moments in the Big Top awakened me to a God who really saw me. I no longer felt lost in a crowd or separate from an indifferent God. I felt known, from my lustful thoughts to the deep insecurities I wrestled with at school. God knew me personally and still wanted to stick around. That was something I would never be able to escape in the years that followed.

Another curious thing at those camps was that I was such a good Christian and it was effortless. At least I was what I thought defined a 'good Christian' at that time. I would wake up before the morning meetings to read my Bible alone in my tent and have deep conversations with the leaders about spiritual things till late at night.

At first when I was back home my whole thinking had changed. Even my mum noticed it, announcing abruptly to my siblings, 'Tim's different.' It was true. I was. I was hungry for God. Sometimes I would wake up and just start meditating on him without even trying to and I would feel guilty when I swore or told a crude joke. But after a while I would forget the camp ever happened. I was back in this uncontrollable dance, pining for acceptance in all kinds of places and grappling with familiar insecurity.

## My dancing days are over . . .

At 16 years old when I finished school and started working in the workshop, the dancing finally stopped. Repeatedly I came home after work feeling wounded, heading straight to my room time and again and laying my soul bare before God because I didn't know who else to turn to. After a while, going up my stairs into my room was reminiscent of returning to the big tent at youth camp with a deep expectation that God himself was there waiting for me. I sensed in my room I had all his attention.

I realised that part of the suffering I was enduring stemmed from the dancing I'd become so accustomed to. I was stuck between camp and school, torn between living for God and fitting in. I knew it would have to stop, that I had to bravely choose to turn my life over to God once and for all, and that year I did. At that time I hadn't learnt all the 'right' prayers that I got burdened with later in life. My growing friendship with God was honest and still had a childlikeness I'm searching to reclaim. I remember when the dancing stopped, church meetings didn't feel the same. Connecting with God in the company of hundreds of others made me feel like I was passionately kissing a girl in public. I wanted to be alone with God, because when I was, it felt like I was being fed a special food that no one else knew about. I felt stronger and more resilient, and after a while I started to crave that space where it was just me and God.

Things changed at the workshop eventually. I told my college teacher about what was happening and she was shocked by how I was being treated. We sat down in the break room and she helped me to hand in my notice and to find a new job. It was a relief to leave, but amidst it all I recognised something powerful had taken place in me. My dancing days were over. I seemed different on the inside; more confident and settled. In that painful time I had discovered a secret, like Lucy when she found the wardrobe that took her into Narnia. The secret was God. But not a sermon about him a preacher shared – I had heard thousands of those already by that point. It wasn't that God changed the situation either, though for a while I wished he had – I daydreamed about God getting revenge on the workshop boss, similar to the film *Bruce Almighty* when Bruce makes Evan Baxter talk gibberish whilst reading the news. But really that didn't matter, because what had happened is I'd found God and something *had* changed, something *within* me, and for that I was eventually grateful.

The mighty God, the maker of heaven and earth, will not be one of many treasures, not even the chief of all treasures. He will be all in all or he will be nothing.

(A. W. Tozer)

\* \* \*

> ## Question
> 
> When was the last time you were honest with God about how you feel? Maybe try today...

_____
_____
_____
_____

## REFLECTION

I know you want to be my all in all or nothing at all
   So blind me like Saul, take me off my horse
Because I want to see you again for who you really are
   I want to love you without any hidden reasons
There isn't certain seasons for loving Jesus
   God himself is the end by which we were all created
It's so blatant I can't escape it

(From 'The Canal' by Timothypoet,
featured on Prayers from the Mountain EP, 2020)

# 2

# WHAT BILLY TAUGHT ME

*My identity as Abba's child is not an abstraction or a tap dance into religiosity. It is the core truth of my existence.*

BRENNAN MANNING

After I escaped the workshop I started a new job with a great company. They had red-printed vans and specialised in completing extensions and loft conversions in people's homes. I felt more like a real tradesman with my own company T-shirt. I much preferred it to working in the same dusty workshop every day, not to mention having a much kinder boss. Since the workshop and the dancing stopped, since I discovered God in my bedroom and that he wasn't just waiting in church meetings and youth camps but also in bedrooms and on building sites, I was addicted to him. From morning cups of tea to cutting insulation, God was consuming my thoughts with a strange joy instead of all the negative comparisons and insecurity I had so often been at war with.

At work I was frequently in the van going to and from jobs and builders' merchants, so I would tear the cardboard lid off boxes of screws and scribble down almost illegible things God was saying to me, tucking the notes into my back pocket to reread later.

A kind builder I worked with, called Matthew, who later became a family friend, was complaining about his health one day. He has Lyme disease and was taking medication that caused warts to appear all over his hands and feet. I told him timidly when we were outside the office one morning that God could heal him. To my surprise he said he wanted me to pray. I mumbled a short prayer, trying not to draw too much attention: 'God, heal Matt's hands, take away these warts.' I quickly moved on, feeling slightly embarrassed.

I had all but forgotten about it until I next saw Matt. He was laughing and shouting something I couldn't hear.

He opened out his hands and shouted 'Look!', walking closer from a distance.

I got nearer and could see the warts had completely gone.

'You healed me,' he said proudly.

## Ross-on-Wye

I'm still doing carpentry today – thankfully Chris back in the workshop was wrong and I completed a three-year apprenticeship. Recently I renovated a whole house, but as I mentioned previously, right up until I left school all I wanted to do was to be a farmer. I guess there's a sense of pride about farming in my family. My grandpa has lived on the same farm in Ross-on-Wye his entire life. He can tell you the dates when trees were planted and the last time the river froze over. The house they live in was built by his grandfather and he bought it with his wife, Patsy, for £5,000 after the Second World War. It's since been a refuge to many: missionaries, ministers and wide extended family from all around the world.

There was quite a significant period of my childhood when there was nowhere else I would rather be than at my grandparents' house on the farm in Ross-on-Wye. Granny and Grandpa's house is called Hillfield. It has a big open fire in the sitting room and an Aga in the kitchen that I would sometimes lean my back against for a quick warming or, when I was feeling especially mischievous, drop spit onto the hot plates and watch it fizz until the heat caused it to disappear. The kitchen window looked out over the garden with a breathtaking view across a valley, a magnolia tree to the right, a chestnut to the left and a weeping willow at the bottom of the lawn sloping down into the woods. The woods sloped even further down to the river, filled with narrow pathways and dens built around fallen trees. In the summer, our many cousins would congregate at Hillfield, swimming in the river and playing games in the woods.

I would always stay in the 'blue room', which is a small room at the front of the house with a large Narnia-like cupboard, but more importantly it was my dad's old room, which made it feel special.

It wasn't just my dad, his brothers and my grandparents that grew up farming; my cousin Billy did too. Billy lived on a small farm called Baysham, made up of red-brick buildings. We have the same great-grandfather, Edward Rudge, who bred pedigree Herefordshire cattle and won shows at the local market. When he retired, he gave my grandpa (Philip), Billy's grandpa (David) and the other brother (Henry) each farms adjoining one another. Billy's family farm was predominantly a sheep farm; at one stage they had almost a thousand sheep. An essential job in the summer for a shepherd is shearing and Billy was the best shearer I knew. I remember eagerly arriving one summer, excited beyond belief by the familiar scenery, and rushing down to the toolshed to witness Billy sharpening the teeth on his clipper. I joined him sometimes when he was shearing. We would load all the gear into his dad's red Land Rover and drive around the country lanes visiting local farmers like Ruth Hanes and John Probert; John lived across the river in Kings Caple. John's daughter fancied Billy, which I always teased him about.

## Billy

I used to stand in awe watching Billy shear sheep. It's like a dance; every single body movement and position of the sheep is choreographed to perfection to keep the sheep's skin taut and the animal relaxed. On the last stroke as the clippers came up through the fleece, it would come loose. At this point I would lunge in, grab the wool and move it away from the board where Billy was shearing so he could move on to the next sheep. My job was wrapping the wool: tearing off the dirty bits, then folding all the edges in, wrapping it up like a blanket and then finally pushing it down into big wool bags. For me, the smell of the oily laminin will forever spark stories and beautiful vivid memories of shearing with Billy.

Billy and I were born a month apart, and every half-term, summer holiday and any other chance I got, I was at the farm with Billy. We referred to 'townies' with contempt, but deep down, though I would never admit it at the time, I knew I was one of them. In the countryside it seemed like the rules were different – I felt free as though we could stumble into an adventure anywhere. Between Baysham, Whitehouse and Hillfield we had almost a thousand acres of land surrounding the River Wye to roam. Baysham, where Billy lived, was a mile's uphill cycle back to Hillfield where I stayed with my grandparents. Every meal was a feast at Gran's and so I would rarely miss lunch, hurrying back on my old bike to be welcomed by Gran's enthusiasm and an array of food lovingly prepared. But the meal quickly devoured, I would rush back on my bike to Baysham, not wanting to miss any important happenings on the farm.

As we both grew up, Billy got increasingly involved with work on his farm. Frankly I don't think there was a moment he contemplated doing anything else. Billy taught me to drive a tractor and then an old Toyota pick-up, and showed me how to hold a gun properly. I looked up to him, not just because of his practical skills, which seemed to come so naturally, but also because of the way he held himself.

I always came away from the farm feeling serious. Life was different on the farm but I had a lot of internal pressures Billy didn't seem to possess. I think I was hard on myself and other people at that time, but Billy wasn't – he was soft and kind. I remember picking apples together in his cider orchard and Billy getting stuck at the top of a tree. We both laughed uncontrollably as he reached desperately for a lower branch. I found a metal hurdle which I frantically braced against the tree to help him get a foothold. He dangled down, stretching, still laughing hysterically, laughing so much he wet himself, which made us both laugh even harder.

At 16 we both had left school for good. Billy carried on farming with his dad and I started my apprenticeship at the workshop. A few years later I was at work in the new company with the kind boss and red vans, standing on top of a scaffold replacing the fascia on a roof, when I got the news. It was cold and wet and I was wearing a big fluorescent coat. My phone rang and it was my gran. When I eventually retrieved my phone, it was far down into my deep pockets beneath old nails and bits of rubbish. I answered but I could hardly hear what she was saying. I tried to position the phone better on my ear but could only hear what sounded like crying and Gran repeating, 'Pray for Billy, he's been in an accident.' I couldn't make out the details of what happened – something about a tractor and a helicopter arriving.

Everything got quiet around me when I put the phone down. I went to the site office with Neil, who I was working with that day, and my boss let me go home. At home I wept in my mum's arms as we found out the news. Billy had died in an accident on the farm. Dad prayed for a miracle to happen but I just kept crying. It felt like the world had stopped or somehow it was carrying on without me in it. At that time I had never lost anyone close to me, not even an older relative, but that terrible day I lost my friend Billy two weeks after his twentieth birthday.

It's hard to describe what grief felt like for me, other than being detached from the world, as though I was hovering above a grey mass, confused about things still moving on. When I opened my journal to write, trying to talk to God, my hand shook and I didn't know what to say. Since working in the workshop it had just flowed. I felt more understood by God than by most of my friends, but at that time my heart felt fragile in a way it never had before, in deep pain hidden somewhere dark. I dreamt at night about being on the farm again with Billy, squeezing through holes in the straw bales and catching sheep in the river meadows.

Over 500 people showed up to Billy's funeral; people from

the young farmers' group he was a part of, friends he sheared for and mates he knew from the pub. I shared a poem about Billy in the service and talked about the time when he wet himself up that apple tree. There wasn't enough space in the little parish church by the river so they put up a big marquee in the grounds and streamed it over. Afterwards, we walked up the hill and buried Billy in a small graveyard next to his grandpa overlooking the river where we had swum so often.

I remember vividly that a few months after Billy passed I met a pastor called Tom Kyle from Chicago for breakfast and he asked me how I was feeling. He didn't know about Billy and I'd grown tired of telling people. I closed my eyes briefly in search of an honest answer, then stared into oblivion. A picture came into my head of me as a climber dangling on the edge of a cliff, holding on with one hand. I'm not sure if it made sense to Tom, but as I said it out loud, it made perfect sense to me. It was certainly how I felt. I told him that all the stuff that surrounded my faith in Jesus had fallen away like loose rocks and it had got really basic again.

I finally wrote something in my journal some days after Billy passed. I looked back at it recently and, with all the painful emotion returning, I saw the small entry that began with 'Dear Abba ...' Reflecting, it's evident that what I found in the days that followed can be summed up in those two words. I found Abba. An Abba that strangely my heart began to trust even more deeply. The Bible refers to God as 'Abba' a lot. It's a Hebrew word which in English translates to something like

'Daddy'. I found the idea of God being my 'Abba' an uncomfortable concept at first. But I think it's because God being 'Daddy' confronted so much of the false theology I had begun sticking to God. All I know is that when Billy died, God showed himself as Abba and that was enough process for a long while.

I recently read something that Charles H. Spurgeon, the great nineteenth-century preacher, wrote in one of his daily readings: 'I have learned to kiss the waves that throw me against the Rock of Ages.' It would be deceitful to tell you I did the same, that I kissed those cruel waves as they threw me up out of my familiar waters, but I do know that I also found myself stranded on the Rock of Ages. For me, it was as if the tide had come in and the sea had risen and there was nowhere else I was brave enough to swim to. I stayed right there, pinned, with no energy to even move a limb. Clinging tightly for dear life to Abba. I had no capacity for lofty debates and discussions about faith; the slightest scent of them would send me spiralling into an anxious abyss. But I'm glad I stayed there, lodged uncomfortably in the arms of Abba.

Somewhere along the way, between the workshop and Billy's death, religion had started to show its head. I couldn't perceive it at the time. I simply remember starting to believe that God had a lot on his plate and it would only be those who could make themselves seen who would get his attention. And of course the best way to make myself seen is surely to perform. But I was shown something different after Billy died. God isn't flicking through his calendar searching for an open day, but instead he is desperately wanting to interrupt and intervene, wanting to weave into every waking and sleeping moment of my life. Wanting in every moment to lead me deeper into being his beloved. Not giving me an answer to why Billy died, but being a faithful rock I can desperately spread out on like a seal. A rock where I was allowed to gasp for breath and shake in my suffering and in my own time discover an even deeper beauty in being here. So I was that seal pinned awkwardly to the rocks for a long while, enjoying amidst the pain, this 'Abba' love that mysteriously began to seep into the deepest places of my heart.

> Charles de Foucauld, the founder of the Little Brothers of Jesus, wrote a single sentence that's had a profound impact on my life. He said, 'The one thing we owe absolutely to God is never to be afraid of anything.' Never to be afraid of anything, even death, which, after all, is but that final breakthrough into the open, waiting, outstretched arms of Abba.
> (Brennan Manning, *The Ragamuffin Gospel*)

## Question

How would you live if you knew you never had to perform to get God's attention?

# 3

# LIGHTEST LOAD

*On the road there's plenty of shade just no place to hide*
  *There's no reason for a disguise*
*No costume that can deceive his eyes*
  *On the road you meet love for the first time*
*Over and over again and where we end he begins*
  *What a paradox, that only those who enter through death can experience such life*
*Like it's falling off the edge, diving in deep that gives reach for the heights*
  *My grip was so tight, but I started learning that his burden is so light*

(From 'The Road' by Timothypoet,
featured on Prayers from the Mountain EP, 2020)

## Heaviness

It was a shock to a lot of people when about six months after Billy passed, and four years after I started my apprenticeship in that workshop and was finally a fully qualified carpenter, I decided to quit my job and move to California to attend

Bethel School of Supernatural Ministry. The tradesmen with the red vans certainly didn't understand what I was doing. I humorously told them it was like Hogwarts, but that raised even more questions which I struggled to answer. But all I knew was there was a growing hunger in me for more of God that I needed to follow.

I remember coming home after completing my first year in the US. I arrived at San Francisco airport, eager to finally be flying back to Blighty to be with my family. I smiled a little as I remembered the panic of the night before: squeezing T-shirts and lots of books frantically into every crack in my suitcase. My gran gave me a lesson when I was a child about how to pack a suitcase properly. She grew up in Zambia and would have to pack frequently for the trips to and from her boarding school in Cape Town, travelling on a long train that drove through the night. She taught me a kind of militant roll that requires a full-body effort but gets you maximum packing space.

Somehow I had forgotten all of it. Now I was standing in the check-out line feeling sheepish in a pair of flip-flops, with a broken zip on one of my suitcases, anxiously trying to stabilise all my belongings. At home I would always make two trips when carrying my coffee and breakfast from the kitchen to the table because it seemed too much, balancing both so early in the morning. Everything is always harder in the morning. My wife Maria and I are both on the same page on that. We have a rule: no talking first thing in the morning, *especially* before coffee. Occasionally I wake a while before Maria and break the rule. She gives me a glare that needs no explanation, reaffirming how important our rule is.

But now it was 6am in the airport and no one knew 'the rule'. I had already been awake for four hours and had spent over three hours in the car on the drive down, making agonising small talk with another student I'd got a lift with. I was attempting to hold my two big suitcases either side of me with my guitar wedged on top of one, my carry-on bag attached to the other, and an over-heavy rucksack pulling me backwards. For a fleeting moment I thought about letting it pull me back, imagining falling and landing into a deep sleep. However, I resurfaced from a half-sleep with the sound of 'Next, please' coming from the desk and I nudged myself forward mechanically. A mixture of tiredness and lack of limbs drove me to adopt this little shuffle, using all my body to slide my belongings closer to the desk.

Now I was at the desk, fearing the worst part of the whole ordeal, the question that every weary traveller dreads. I had been there so many times I knew it was coming, like a script. I handed over my passport. The check-in official tapped on her keyboard, then looked up and asked, 'Are you carrying too much weight?'

'I hope not,' I responded, laughing nervously and smiling through my fear.

She laughed too and I looked anxiously at the scales. She

motioned for me to hand her my bags and I reluctantly placed the first onto the scales, mustering up all the energy I had left in an attempt to make the bag look as light as possible. Not that it helped.

She handed me the bag back immediately and said with a sort of smug satisfaction, 'This bag is too heavy. You need to get rid of some weight.'

I say she was smug, but maybe she wasn't. Everyone just seems smug to me when I've had too little sleep, like I'm the only bird without a worm and the whole world knows it.

I sat on the floor just beside the check-in desk with an open bag trying to decide what to throw out and what to wear. At first I lifted up one side of the suitcase to try and stop people in the queue from seeing my underwear, but after a while I lost all dignity. I started pulling things out and digging through my belongings like a mole, trying to find something heavy. I held up a book in one hand and a hoodie in the other, closing my eyes and trying to think about which of them weighed more. It's amazing the things you can throw away when you have to.

I had read about a Scotsman on a flight to Edinburgh from Paris. He was carrying too much weight so he proceeded to put on every T-shirt he owned, 15 in total.

The thing is, strange as it sounds, sometimes I hear God like that woman from check-in and he asks the same question:

# LIGHTEST LOAD

'Are you carrying too much weight?' Because I am, all the time. Especially lately. I'm not sure when it started; I don't remember feeling heavy as a child but it seems like it's something that built as I grew older. I'm not talking about luggage now or extra pounds on my waist. Let me be perfectly clear that when I say 'I don't remember feeling heavy as a child' I'm not talking about being a bit podgy. It's a different type of weight I'm getting at, not a physical one; more of an internal heaviness in my soul. When it's really bad, it's as if there's a pressure pulling me underwater, making it hard to breathe and think straight.

I was feeling heavy recently. I don't know any other way to describe it other than this image in my head: I'm moving slowly through thick mud, not in a fun way, like when I was a kid in welly boots, but in a desperate way as if I need to get to the other side because my life depends on it; but my feet are trapped. When I get caught there, I start questioning everything and think crazy thoughts like my life has no meaning and purpose.

I have this scripture from Matthew's Gospel that I typed up stuck on my wall. I couldn't get it out of my head for months. It says:

> Come to me, all you who are weary and burdened, and I will give you rest. Take my yoke upon you and learn from me, for I am gentle and humble in heart, and you will find rest for your souls. For my yoke is easy and my burden is light.
>
> (Matthew 11:28–30 NIV)

I seemed to carry a measure of heaviness a lot. Maybe it's because I'm hard on myself and put too much on my plate. But there is always a cost to carrying too much weight, just like when you overpack your suitcase. I learned in San Fran airport you either pay the price or find a way to get rid of the weight.

## Shrek the lost sheep – letting go of independence

I find it interesting that in the Bible Jesus constantly refers to himself as our Shepherd. I read a story about a sheep called Shrek. He was found in the mountains of New Zealand after spending six years wandering the hills, living in caves and on mountaintops away from the rest of the flock. It sounds dramatic but sometimes I feel like Shrek: lost, confused and too far from the Shepherd. Shrek left the flock, so he never went home to the farm at the bottom of the valley for the winter and he didn't receive his yearly shear in the summer. I started thinking about how an animal that fears independence got so lost. Did he get separated by a predator? Or maybe he saw greener grass in the distance and, before he knew it, he couldn't see his friends? More than that, I'm amazed at how long he stayed lost, carrying so much weight on his back he could never get rid of on his own.

I know independence feels good for a while. I remember learning to ride a bicycle for the first time and how incredible it felt leaving my dad's side and riding without his help. I think we all grow up with that compulsion to do it alone. Even after we meet God it seems hard to shake. I also remember, during that first year at Bethel ministry school in America, having a light-bulb realisation in the car park at church. I suddenly realised that the whole way in which I had been approaching God was about getting to a place where I no longer needed him. It sounds strange to say, but it was a huge revelation to me. Growing up in this world seems to be all about becoming less dependent on people and systems and more dependent on ourselves. So it's no wonder we do the same with God and think spiritual maturity is having the answers and solutions on our own. I get it – we shouldn't be living at home till we're 40, still asking our mum when dinner is ready. We should want to forge our own path. But I also believe now that true life, meaning and purpose cannot be found alone, independently.

John writes in John 1:4, 'In him [Jesus] was life'.

Jeanne Guyon, a French seventeenth-century mystic, said, 'He alone has life. All other creatures have "borrowed life".'

We were made to be constantly and intimately connected to God; that is our highest calling because when we are connected we enter into true life. Not so I can get somewhere impressive or finally be the man who can do it alone. That's what I finally realised in the car park in America – relationship with Jesus isn't a means to an end; it *is* the end. Friendship with Jesus is the whole story.

## Spirit of heaviness

Isaiah the prophet says in Isaiah 63 that God wants to give us a garment of praise in exchange for the spirit of heaviness. He calls heaviness a spirit and an evil one at that. It doesn't come with the job and it's not part of life – it's a spirit! I've often heard the phrases 'That's life' or 'It's just part of life' when referring to this weariness and heaviness, but I started thinking: is it really just part of life? Jesus certainly doesn't seem to think it is. I'm not saying life isn't hard and chaotic. I'm not saying there isn't work to be done which comes with responsibility and stress. I just don't think the weight of the world should be on our shoulders. In moments of clarity I can see how dangerous it is; how this spirit of heaviness is determined to suck all the joy out of existing, until I simply don't want to do it any more.

Again, this is what Jesus said in Matthew 11. I think Eugene Peterson puts it best in *The Message*:

> Are you tired? Worn out? Burned out on religion? Come to me. Get away with me and you'll recover your life. I'll show you how to take a real rest. Walk with me and work with me – watch how I do it. Learn the unforced rhythms of grace. I won't lay anything heavy or ill-fitting on you. Keep company with me and you'll learn to live freely and lightly.
> (Matthew 11:28–30 MSG)

Jesus is saying, 'If you walk with me in a state of dependence, I will show you how these things that appear to be so heavy need not weigh you down. Follow me and I will show you the light way.' But to follow him you can't live like Shrek alone on the mountain. You have to surrender your independent life and your lone search for any greener grass there might be and give yourself over to the Shepherd. I know I have to keep coming off the mountain, where I get so busy trying to spin the plates and make it all happen by myself, and remind myself that 'all life apart from Christ is borrowed'.

When Shrek was discovered, at first people didn't even recognise him as a sheep. He had been lost for so long that all that excess wool meant he looked more like a large boulder than an animal. They took him back home to the farm and removed his fleece, which weighed 41 kilograms, the weight of an average sheep. Shrek broke the world record for the heaviest fleece ever shorn. He had been walking around the hills of New Zealand carrying his body weight in wool.

## Letting go of extra weight

Maria and I went to Northern Ireland a few years ago for a friend's wedding. We had only booked for carry-on bags so we wheeled right in. No anxious weighing of bags or awkward luggage shuffles like in San Fran, just a short queue before boarding. We stood looking through the glass at the plane and chatted about what we wanted to do when we got to Belfast. There was a guy standing behind us in the queue who made me and Maria laugh. He was in his late twenties, wearing sports shorts and a T-shirt, earpods in and holding his phone and passport together in one hand. No wheelie bag, not even a rucksack, just a phone and a passport. He looked as if he had just finished playing tennis and was in the line for a smoothie, not queuing up to board a two-hour flight. Maria and I debated about who he was, imagining he was so rich he just showed up at airports and bought new clothes at his destination, just for the thrill.

We looked ahead as the queue quickly moved forward and spotted the staff pulling people aside and directing them to a woman with a card machine. Suddenly we realised that they were charging people who had a personal item as well as their carry-on bag. Once again the anxiety hit. I took my bag off my back, contemplating the viable options. I started turning the rucksack like a jigsaw piece; laying it on top of my carry-on trying to imagine the best way to force it all in. The closer we got to the desk the more desperate I got, settling in to my fate. In true Ryanair fashion I expected to pay the same price for my extra bag as I'd paid for the entire flight. But as we approached the desk something totally unexpected happened.

The tennis guy behind us put his hand on my wheelie bag and whispered 'I've got you' under his breath like he was in MI5. He then walked away to the desk on the left, whilst we headed to the right to check in. It all happened so quickly that I didn't know how to react. The tennis guy had just taken my bag! But as we walked through without any issue it suddenly all clicked. Tennis guy didn't have a bag of his own so he took my extra one as his. Genius. Once we were on the plane, he nonchalantly lifted my bag up into the overhead luggage space and made his way to his seat. I felt like I was in my own movie. *This stuff never happens to me*, I thought, as I squeezed past Maria to the window seat. It didn't matter that it probably only would have cost us £40; we both felt like we'd won the lottery. Well, maybe not the National Lottery but definitely a lucrative scratch card or one of those free round-the-world trips no one ever wins.

## Jesus is the load lifter

The thing about travelling with too much weight, or even an extra bag, is that if you aren't willing to repack your bag on the airport floor (which I totally understand) you have to pay a fee for the additional kilos. But isn't this exactly the message of Jesus? He is like the tennis guy who, without making a scene, comes slowly from behind and approaches me (tired, anxious and fed up) and says 'I got you'. All I have to do is let go of my baggage. Just let go. Jesus isn't just the check-in woman asking if I'm carrying too much weight; he's also the cool tennis guy who, whilst I'm anxiously wondering how I'm going to pay, comes through and gently takes my stuff from me.

Honestly I think deep down Shrek wanted to be found, wanted to come home, wanted to leave the nomad life and return to dependency upon the Shepherd. Only then could he part with the heavy thick fleece that he'd been lugging around. I don't want the weight any more either, even the stuff people say *should* be heavy. If Jesus said when we come to him we can let go of heavy things, then that must mean all of it. The pressure to make ends meet, my fear about the future, and the countless thoughts that so often plague my mind, the things I need to do and things that I haven't done. I'm convinced Jesus is the Good Shepherd and he wants me to come home and part ways with all heaviness. I feel sad that I have lived so often out in the fields, searching like Shrek for something better, when all that I ever needed was at home in Jesus. But lately I've been living there more, returning to that quiet intimate place with Jesus, the source of all true life, knowing that his first agenda is always to unburden me from any weight.

> Come to me, all you who are weary and burdened, and I will give you rest. Take my yoke upon you and learn from me, for I am gentle and humble in heart, and you will find rest for your souls. For my yoke is easy and my burden is light.
> (Matthew 11:28–30)

## Questions

- Are you feeling heavy or weighed down? If you are, write down on a piece of paper the things making you feel heavy. Maybe it's pressure from work, problems with friendships, or people's expectations of you.

- Write down any reflections you have on this statement from Jesus: 'Come to me, all you who are weary and burdened, and I will give you rest.'

LIGHTEST LOAD

_____
_____
_____
_____

## A PRAYER FOR THE HEAVY-HEARTED

Lord, often I've tried so hard not to involve you and to do it all alone, but even my greatest attempts couldn't lift this weight. I tried going my own way but now I'm turning and I'm moving towards yours. I've found no answer for the critic, no remedy for my doubt, no smart scheme that can save me; without you my river always returns to drought. I'm placing my feet on the road again and asking you to take me home. Move me swiftly away from anxious thoughts. I want to breathe in like it's a gift again and be like a ship surrendered to the sea. Please, Jesus, lead me into your lightness today. Free me from the burden to achieve and make something of myself. Set me free, cut me loose now, I pray.

# 4
# RADICAL ROOT

*Name of Jesus! Highest name!*
*Name that earth and heaven adore!*
*From the heart of God it came,*
*Leads me to God's heart once more.*

*Name of Jesus! Living tide!*
*Days of drought for me are past;*
*How much more than satisfied*
*Are the thirsty lips at last.*

*Name of Jesus! Dearest name!*
*Bread of Heaven, and balm of love,*
*Oil of gladness, surest claim*
*To the treasures stored above.*

*Jesus gives forgiveness free,*
*Jesus cleanses all my stains,*
*Jesus gives his life to me,*
*Jesus always he remains.*

*Only Jesus! Fairest name!*
*Life, and rest and peace, and bliss;*
*Jesus, evermore the same,*
*He is mine, and I am his.*
(Hymn by Gerhard Tersteegen, 1697–1769)

A few years ago I was cutting down a tree outside my house. It was a large, bushy tree that shaded a considerable part of the garden and was peculiarly placed in front of the window of the living room, casting a continual shadow inside the house. I found old flowerpots and other random items hidden deep inside as I began to cut the branches off and take the tree back to a bare trunk. I stood back and stared at what was left. The now unimpressive, bare trunk of a tree weirdly put an image of a poodle with a newly cut coat into my head and made me smile, almost embarrassed for the tree. I began digging round the base, exposing roots and hacking them off with a spade as I went. I felt like one of those boys from the movie *Holes*, digging desperately for a lost treasure. Once the tree was loose enough I started rocking it back and forth to break the roots, further enjoying the strangely satisfying feeling as the roots cracked with every different angle.

That night, Maria and I had some friends over for dinner, so I had to reluctantly leave the tree without finishing the job. We sat out in the garden with our friends, chatting, with a big bonfire burning the branches and other bits of wood I had found around the garden. But the tree hadn't left the back of my mind. After people had gone, I looked over at my brother and with a few words exchanged we both went over to finish the job. We rocked the tree back and forth for hours until it was dangling like a baby tooth, barely hanging on but still stubbornly refusing to let go. It got darker and darker but it was impossible for either of us to leave. After a while, using the torch on my phone, we investigated the roots. Steve pushed the tree to one side and I bent down in the soil. I realised there was a big root right in the middle of the tree; the root was going straight down, anchoring the tree into the ground. We found an axe in the shed and set on that middle root like madmen. In an instant the tension released and the tree fell like Goliath. Exhausted, we dropped our tools and rushed inside without any delay, arguing about who had given it the last blow.

I was telling my dad about it because he's a gardener; his party trick is knowing the Latin name of any tree in sight. I was intrigued about the middle root and he explained to me as if it was completely obvious that almost all trees have one. It's the first root to grow, he said, going straight down, preventing the tree from falling and enabling it to find water and nutrition to help it grow. I went to the redwood forests in Eureka, California, a few years ago. I think I spent the whole time awestruck. I had never seen such enormous trees. I heard they filmed *Jurassic Park* in the area, which made the whole experience even more surreal. I learned some of those trees are 2,000 years old and stand 400 feet (120 metres) tall. I stood at the bottom of one and stared up, enjoying the feeling of being so minute in comparison. There's a certain place where you can drive through the root of a tree that bridges across the road. I started thinking about those redwoods as my dad explained more details that went over my head, and I laughed a little as I imagined myself and Steve trying to take out one of those massive middle roots!

After that conversation with Dad, it struck me that maybe as human beings we are designed to have a middle root too, clearly not a physical one, but a spiritual one that also grounds and sustains us, stops us from collapsing when the winds blow and life seems to get chaotic. Shortly afterwards, one morning when I was reading Mark 3, it was as if God was pointing and saying 'This is it.' That middle root, the one that should be growing the deepest and furthest down.

> Jesus went up on a mountainside and called to him those he wanted, and they came to him. He appointed twelve – designating them apostles – that they might be with him and that he might send them out to preach and to have authority to drive out demons.
>
> (Mark 3:13–15)

In the passage, Jesus the rabbi calls these twelve men he has individually encountered to go with him and ultimately become his disciples. They begin climbing a mountain, oblivious to what they are walking into or what following this rabbi will look like. But on the mountain, where Jesus was alone with his new friends and no one else could hear, privately he asked them two things which set the record straight and would soon change their lives for ever. You can read it in the passage. First, he asked them to *be with him*. This is very significant. He could have said anything, but that was his first request. Then Jesus told them they would be sent out into the world to do all kinds of wonderful, miraculous things.

Shortly after I uprooted the tree in my garden, our friends Marcus and Amanda asked me to speak at their wedding in the Lake District. When they asked, I contemplated my one year of marriage experience and debated if it would be dishonouring to say no. It wasn't that I didn't want to; I just wasn't sure I had anything to say. I said yes anyway and shared this story about cutting down the tree and how I think we are all supposed to have our own middle root, one that grounds and sustains us. After the service in the church we went to the reception in an old barn. They had a big oak table in the foyer with an amazing Mediterranean spread of meats and cheeses, all my wife's favourite things. Maria enjoys picking at food; I call her a grazer.

A woman was looking at me from across the room as we were standing and eating and I could tell she wanted to talk to me. I walked over a little awkwardly and she told me she was from Southampton and that she liked what I'd shared. Smiling eagerly, she asked if I knew what the name of that middle root is. I told her I didn't, intrigued. Still smiling, she told me it was called the *radical root*. I'm not sure how she knew that, but it made me smile too. I believe our middle root is the pursuit of being with Jesus. It's our radical root and Jesus' first request of his disciples.

After some tree research (never thought I would say that) I found out that, interestingly and quite uniquely, banana trees don't have a radical root. In fact, banana trees grow the same amount in their first six months as an oak tree will grow in six years. At around 12 months a banana plant should bear its first fruit, whereas an oak tree starts producing acorns when it's about 40 years old. In fact its most productive years are between 60 and 110 years old.

The first request Jesus made to his friends in Mark 3 before they committed to follow him was 'Will you be with me?' The implications were: If you commit to being with me it will cost you everything. My friend Josh Luke Smith puts it beautifully when he says, 'It costs us everything we don't want to be.' But being with Jesus would also cause them to become 'oaks' that would start something in this life that outlived them and produced fruit all over the world.

In that light, truth be told, I think it is *radical* to be with Jesus, especially in this modern age when there is such a pressure to instantaneously have something to show for every bit of effort we apply to life. But the long-term truth is this: really big trees that have roots that extend wide and deep grow taller and more beautiful than banana plants could ever dream of. Big trees, like the ones in the redwood forests I placed my hands on, have spanned countless eras. They have couples' names engraved in them and swings attached to their branches. Big trees, the ones that last, have a deep radical root – and I want one too.

> He appointed twelve – designating them apostles – **that they might be with him.**
>
> (Mark 3:14, my emphasis)

When I was cutting down that tree in my garden and God started speaking to me about this verse, I hadn't long been back from America. I received far more than I will be able to express during that time away at Bethel School of Supernatural Ministry. I met Maria, now my wife. But when I returned after those three years I was in some ways shocked to be confronted with the same simple discovery I had experienced in the workshop and when Billy died. I hadn't had some new epiphany or reached a spiritual climax as I perhaps thought I would. Quickly, fresh back from California, still grappling with new time zones and unfriendly Brits, I had a sober, deep conviction that what my heart desired more than anything was to know God. To really know him deeply and honestly and to live a life surrendered to that desire. I started to see clearly what I think God had been trying to show me all along, that knowing him started with learning to *be with him* as top priority. It was as if God was focusing me like an athlete and setting my course, just as he did with the disciples on that mountain. Asking me humbly to accept that being with him would trump all else, that it would be the desire that overshadows all others. 'Will you be with me?' I felt his words ringing again through my being with a sense of longing and love that came from his heart.

After that I began asking different questions, such as 'What does it mean to be with Jesus, whom most of the time I cannot see, and how do I practise being with him today?' I realised quickly that being with Jesus isn't a whimsical idea. It can't be. It has to be fought for and comes with great resistance. In the rest of this short book we begin more intentionally exploring these questions and others that surround this sacred question Jesus whispered to his disciples on a mountainside: 'Will you be with me?'

## Questions

- Why do you think, out of everything Jesus could have asked his friends, that the first thing he said was 'Will you be with me'?

- What questions arise in your heart when you think about being with Jesus?

## PRAYER FOR THOSE LONGING FOR THE LORD

Father, it's so easy to be blinded by the lights. To be dazed and confused in this world of information and instant gratification. I know I've danced to the music and performed on cue, not because I had to but because I wanted to. I love the buzz. But like a sugar high, I always come down and I'm left feeling empty. People's praise never fills me like I think it will; but Father today, deep within me is a longing for you. I am surrounded by temptation – to overwork, overthink, meet more needs and make more money. But Father, here I am today confessing that I am in need. I need courage and new strength to leave the crowd and temporary rewards for a treasure locked up in your heart. Take me to the mountain where it's just me and you and I know for sure that I am enough.

## SECTION TWO
# Being with Jesus

# 5
# LOS ANGELES

*Once you become aware that the main business you are here for is to know God, most of life's problems fall into place of their own accord.*

(J. I. PACKER)

In 2018 over the Christmas holidays, Maria and I went on a road trip with her family down the west coast of the United States. We started with a few days in Redding, California, where Maria and I met at Bethel School of Supernatural Ministry. We returned to all our favourite spots such as the bluffs with a view of the Sacramento river, enjoyed Theory Coffee again and reminisced with old friends. Redding is in Northern California, so after five days we travelled nine hours on big open highways down through California to Los Angeles where we arranged to meet the rest of the family.

When we arrived it was bright and warm. The streets were filled with people in beach clothes, quite an odd contrast to our usual cold English Christmases. On Christmas Eve we walked to the Observatory at sunset, where you have a perfect view of the famous Hollywood sign, whilst packs of coyotes howled across the city. It was very atmospheric.

## Runyon Canyon

Maria's parents had arranged for us to go on a hiking tour of LA on Boxing Day which would give us amazing views across the city with trails winding round some of LA's most exclusive houses. The unique part of the tour, however, was that we would be walking with rescue dogs. The picture on the advert showed dogs of all kinds trekking up the beautiful hills. This may sound curious but Mandy, Maria's mum, is such an avid dog-lover that it wouldn't surprise me if she'd found the only tour in LA that involved dogs. Actually, all Maria's family love dogs and, given that Maria and her sister Jen have a dislike of walking, it was probably the only way Mandy could convince them to go on a hike the day after Christmas.

We all waited eagerly at the entrance of the park, slightly bewildered by the unusual Christmas sun kissing our skin. I was expecting it to be like a scene out of *101 Dalmatians* with a guy appearing in the distance, struggling, holding three dogs on leads in each hand. But when the tour guide finally arrived we didn't know it was him; he approached us from the other side of the street as if he knew us. He reached where we were standing and quickly introduced himself as Ryan. He was so happy and chatty, as most Americans are. He asked us where we were from and we told him 'England'. He did his best English accent on cue and questioned us about why we call the day after Christmas 'Boxing Day'.

Next he explained all the possible wildlife we might encounter as we hiked up the trail, which made Grant's ears prick up (Grant is Maria's dad) because he is obsessed with birds. But as the chit-chat continued we became more and more confused about where the dogs were. I stared over the road, thinking they must be packed in the back of his car across the street.

Finally Maria's dad mustered up the courage to ask Ryan very politely, 'This is the hike with rescue dogs, isn't it?'

'Yes, yes, no, this is it,' said Ryan, proceeding to tell us how his rescue dog couldn't make it because he was unwell, taking out his phone and flicking lovingly through the album of his dog. As he showed Mandy, I turned round so no one could see me silently laughing at the awkwardness.

Another couple showed up, looking as confused as we had been. I watched the whole exchange unfold. 'This is the dog tour?' they asked tentatively. Ryan assured them again it was and passed them the photos of his dog with the same explanation.

The funniest part of it was that he was not abashed at all by the blatant misrepresentation. I felt bad for Mandy because she was so excited to see some dogs. I think Ryan could tell we were disappointed. As we set off he tried his best to cheer us up and assured us we would see plenty of dogs as we walked, which tickled me even more.

So off we went on our dog hike, with no dogs. We walked and laughed a little to one another when Ryan wasn't looking, making our way up Runyon Canyon towards the Hollywood hills. There was a street with huge, beautiful houses that lots of famous people live in. Ryan pointed to one and said it belonged to Britney Spears. Someone else mentioned that Justin Bieber walked there frequently and went to a café just round the corner. I tried to convince Maria and the rest of her family that we should check it out. I follow Justin Bieber on Instagram a lot; I watched his stories about Sushi and Tuna, his Savannah cats, and his wife Hailey. It's embarrassing, but sometimes I have dreams that Justin and I are friends. I do think Justin would really like me if he met me. I have to remind myself internally: *Tim, you are not actually Justin's friend*; otherwise I confuse Maria by dropping his name into conversation as if he's one of the guys. I guess the intriguing and kind of scary point I'm trying to make is that it's possible to know all about someone but not actually know them in the slightest. I can follow Justin on social media, watch all the interviews he's done, listen to all his music and even have a friendship with someone who knows him. But honestly, until we spend time together, clearly our friendship is an illusion. And when I say 'spend time together', I'm not just talking about bumping into him 'accidentally' in his favourite café (I may or may not have considered this); I need to spend consistent time with him before I can say I know Justin and he knows me. That's probably very obvious and basic, but it's helpful for emphasising something significant.

## Ginosko or oida?

As I stated at the end of the last chapter, the practice of being with Jesus is driven to a large extent by a desire to know God, but even saying that can be confusing if we don't determine what knowing God actually means. I think it's important to say, despite its simplicity, the reality is that like many people in our lives, it's possible to know all *about* God but never actually honestly *know* him. J. I. Packer says in his book *Knowing God*: 'A little bit of knowledge of God is worth more than a great deal of knowledge about him.'

So what is the difference between knowledge of God and knowledge about him? In the early days whilst I was still dancing with God, I looked on with jealousy at other people's connection with him with a sinking sense that my own friendship with Jesus was superficial. Equivalent to stalking Justin on Instagram, I had a few scriptures memorised, I knew all the stories, and I even heard other passionate people share about what he's like and nodded and said 'Amen'. But I never actually knew God for myself. This is important to accept because it's the honest, personal knowing of him that our hearts so deeply long for, not just being one of his 'fans'. Listen to what Jesus says in Matthew's Gospel:

> Many will say to me on that day, 'Lord, Lord, did we not prophesy in your name and in your name drive out demons and perform many miracles?' Then I will tell them plainly, 'I never knew you ...' (Matthew 7:22–23)

It's difficult for me to read those words without a slight cold chill reaching the spine. I can't imagine anyone wanting to be the one Jesus says 'I never knew you' to.

The word 'knew' used in this verse is *ginosko*, a Greek word which is often translated in the Bible as 'know' or 'known'. But 'know' doesn't really do justice to the word *ginosko*, especially because another Greek word, *oida*, is also commonly translated as 'know' in the Bible. Confusing, right?

The word *ginosko* best defined would be something like 'a personal, intimate and experiential knowing' whereas *oida* is quite differently defined as 'understanding with the mind'.

So you can see they are quite different in their implications. So often as followers of Jesus, we are driven by the *oida* type of knowing God – learning and understanding – which in itself isn't wrong, but as J. I. Packer says, we are being sold short if we are content to stay there. Some people spend their whole lives camped in a *oida* type of knowing, unaware there is much more fulfilling knowledge of God available to them. The word *ginosko* is always relational – it's about knowing through experience; whereas *oida* is knowledge through observation. God doesn't want observers or Instagram followers; he wants to be known up close, relationally. He wants us to be near enough that we care deeply about what he feels.

Jesus states plainly in Matthew 7:22 that it's possible to even work and serve God's mission faithfully but never actually know him in the way he so desires for us. In the next chapter, we will take another look at that passage in Mark 3 and how the first 12 disciples sought to 'ginosko' God.

> **Question**                                                      ?
>
> How do you understand the difference between a ginosko and oida way of knowing God?

_____
_____
_____

## PRAYER

God, I want to know you. Your nuances, the cadence in your voice, the way you say things, not just what you say. My eyes have been opened to the power locked up in an uncomfortable, intimate knowing of you and now I'll never settle for lesser lovers like information and mental understanding. I want to be intertwined with you so our lines blur and it's impossible to know where you end and I begin. I want to be one with you, not a fan or follower.

# 6

# BODY ODOUR

*Let us occupy ourselves entirely in knowing God. The more we know Him, the more we will desire to know Him. As love increases with knowledge, the more we know God, the more we will truly love Him. We will learn to love Him equally in times of distress or in times of great joy.*

BROTHER LAWRENCE

I'm awake now, though I still slumber. I'm alive with a fierce and sometimes feeble, yet ever-present conviction that knowing God is everything. The true treasure of this life. Here it is again:

> Jesus went up on a mountainside and called to him those he wanted, and they came to him. He appointed twelve – designating them apostles – that they might be with him and that he might send them out to preach and to have authority to drive out demons.
>
> (Mark 3:13–15)

It's important to understand that Jesus didn't arrive on earth to form a new religion. His mission wasn't even to establish something new. Jesus came to proclaim to the world that he was the way to the one true God, Yahweh, the God of Abraham, Isaac and Jacob. From Abraham to the exodus, from David to the exile, and onwards through 400 years of silence between the Old and New Testaments, Jesus was always the fulfilment of the law and the image of the invisible God. The conclusion to all the Jewish context. There can't be a much more consistent message that Jesus seemed to communicate to his disciples than his purpose to reveal his Father.

> Jesus said … 'I am the way, the truth, and the life. No one comes to the Father except through Me. If you had known Me, you would have known My Father also; and from now on you know Him and have seen Him.'
>
> Philip said to Him, 'Lord, show us the Father, and it is sufficient for us.'
>
> Jesus said to him, 'Have I been with you so long, and yet you have not known Me, Philip? He who has seen Me has seen the Father; so how can you say, "Show us the Father"? Do you not believe that I am in the Father, and the Father in Me? The words that I speak to you I do not speak on My own *authority*; but the Father who dwells in Me does the works. Believe Me that I *am* in the Father and the Father in Me, or else believe Me for the sake of the works themselves.'
>
> (John 14:6–11 NKJV)

Jesus affirms to his friends over and over that they knew the nature and character of God more than anyone. Why? Because, as he tells them, **'you've been with me …'**

## The Twelve

Throughout Jesus' ministry from the age of 30 to 33, the 12 disciples were with him, but not as his entourage or groupies; instead they were like family, living awkwardly close to one another's lives.

'Discipleship' isn't a term we hear very often, apart from when it's used by church people, so its true definition can sometimes become a little muddy. A term which is comparable and, in many ways, reflects the heart of what it means to be a disciple is 'apprentice'. I am very united to the process of apprenticeships, having completed my own over a period of three years. An apprenticeship today is about shadowing a skilled person to learn a skill (for me that was construction), but it's also in a more nuanced sense about reflecting the manner in which the teacher holds himself or herself whilst completing those skills. This can't be as easily articulated or written up on paper. But for example, I shadowed a senior tradesman and learned woodwork skills but also how to relate to people professionally, such as customers and colleagues, how to remedy mistakes and how to carry a sense of confidence about my ability to complete tasks. Those latter elements aren't so much taught as 'caught' from simply being around a senior tradesman. That's much of the reason why I experienced such turmoil at the beginning in my first job, when I was working in the workshop. I was positioned to emulate someone who had great woodworking abilities but a character and manner I little desired to embody.

An apprenticeship to a rabbi in Jesus' time was similar but actually with even deeper significance. These days there is a growing demand for apprenticeship. I previously talked about how I sent piles of letters to woodworking firms with only one reply, but the Jewish process was far more rigorous. After a young Jewish boy's Bar Mitzvah, which marked the point when he entered into manhood at around the age of 12, he would start learning the family trade, such as fishing or woodwork. From there only the best students would enter the Beth Midrash, which was essentially secondary school for Jews, where they were taught further application from the Torah by local rabbis. After that, some exceptional Beth Midrash students – the select few – would get to follow a rabbi.

Following a rabbi was a high honour, comparable to getting into a prestigious university; it was the deepest aspiration of a young Jew. But a *talmid*, or disciple as we translate it, was not simply a student; they were not aiming to learn something from the rabbi in order to pass a test, for instance how to hang a door or cut a roof. Being a talmid is more than that; it was all about becoming like their rabbi. Because of this, most students watched and sought out the rabbis they wished to follow. If a student wanted to follow a particular rabbi, he would simply ask that rabbi if he might 'follow' him. The rabbi would consider the student's potential to become like him and whether the young man would make the necessary commitment. It was to be expected that most students would be turned away. Some of course were also invited by a rabbi to 'follow me'. This spoke deeply of the rabbi's belief in their potential and ultimate commitment to become like him.

Interestingly, it's widely acknowledged that the majority of the disciples Jesus chose to follow him had not attended Beth Midrash and probably had given up hope of ever hearing a rabbi say those words: 'Follow me.' In other words, Jesus didn't take the most educated, cream-of-the-crop students, as the other rabbis did. He chose dropouts, including fishermen and a tax collector. But nevertheless, he chose 12 men to begin a life-changing apprenticeship, to shadow Jesus, the great rabbi, hoping to become, in a holistic way, like him. Wherever he went, they went, watching, learning, eating together, travelling together and ministering together. They were put to use administering crowds and supporting Jesus, but their primary, most critical mission was simply with open hearts to be with him.

Clearly, Jesus' teaching and training of his disciples looked a lot different from that of other rabbis. Jesus had awakened them to the seemingly backwards kingdom of Yahweh, flipping everything they grew up believing about God on its head by taking them to towns they had always been forbidden to go to and performing astonishing miracles on the holy sabbath. But after only three years together, already Jesus began preparing his friends for his departure.

'I'm going away to make a place ready for you,' Jesus told his disciples (see John 14:2). Understandably, this made no sense at that time – how could it? But to complicate matters further, Jesus also assured them, 'I will always be with you, even to the end of the age' (see Matthew 28:20).

Was he going or staying? How could he be leaving, yet continue to be with them?

I don't know at what moment the penny dropped and it all began to make sense to the disciples, but essentially Jesus told them that being with him, and him being with them, would continue for the rest of their earthly lives. One day they would die and leave this earth and the joy of John 14:2 would be manifested: they would indeed be united with Jesus in the flesh, able to touch his beard and feel the weight of his arms wrap around their body. But until then, in this awkward yet beautiful place in between, Jesus, their rabbi, would continue to be with them no matter what. Even after Jesus died, was resurrected and then ascended, their apprenticeship hadn't finished, though it was about to look a lot different. Being with Jesus would continue to be their life's work.

## A new way of being

> After his suffering, [Jesus] presented himself to them and gave many convincing proofs that he was alive. He appeared to them over a period of forty days and spoke about the kingdom

of God. On one occasion, while he was eating with them, he gave them this command: 'Do not leave Jerusalem, but wait for the gift my Father promised, which you have heard me speak about. For John baptised with water, but in a few days you will be baptised with the Holy Spirit.'

(Acts 1:3–5)

I am going to send you what my Father has promised; but stay in the city until you have been clothed with power from on high.

(Luke 24:49)

At the beginning of Acts and the end of Luke, we see Jesus again talking about his departure and pleading with his friends: 'Don't go anywhere until you have received the Holy Spirit.' Obviously from our perspective I'm so glad they didn't. In Acts 2, we read the story of Pentecost, when 120 believers gathered as Jesus had instructed, waiting to get filled with the Holy Spirit. Ultimately this is a historic, powerful marker in time, when a whole new way of being with Jesus was made possible. Not just for the 12 disciples but for 120 people, and all those who would follow and respond to the rabbi's words 'Follow me'. Suddenly, not only Jesus' original friends but also everyone who received the Holy Spirit could be with Jesus in this mystical, spiritual way.

## A gate called 'Beautiful'
After those believers encountered Jesus, they began going everywhere and telling people the good news: Jesus of Nazareth, the

carpenter's son, who was killed at the hands of the Jews but raised to life miraculously, had changed everything. He was and is the promised Messiah, Son of Man, Son of God, written about for centuries, and he had revealed a whole new way of living. And it was a better way, one that Abraham and David had dreamed of. The followers of Jesus said to people: If you turn your lives radically towards the one true God, by accepting Jesus as the promised Messiah, through the Holy Spirit, you can be with God, not just in temples but also around meal tables, on fishing boats and on the road. They could be with him all the time, and if they were with him, they would become like him too.

One story documented of those early days, which excites something deep in me, is when Peter and John encountered a man who had been disabled from birth. You can find the story in Acts 3 and 4. This disabled man was brought to sit and beg every day at a gate called 'Beautiful', which was on the way to the temple in Jerusalem. Peter and John saw him sitting on the ground in the dust and blistering sun and approached him. Remember, they both understood, because of what happened at Pentecost, that the one true God wasn't waiting for them at the temple where they would pray, but that through the Holy Spirit, Jesus was actively with them. Arguably, Peter and John knew better than anyone what it was like to be with Jesus. Self-confessed, Jesus was always about the Father's business. Wherever they followed him, unpredictable, weird, miraculous things happened. At Beautiful Gate the disabled man asked them for money, which they didn't have, but they gave what they did have, uttered the name of Jesus and told the man to walk!

> Taking him by the right hand, he helped him up, and instantly the man's feet and ankles became strong. He jumped to his feet and began to walk.
>
> (Acts 3:7–8)

The religious people, the priests and the Sadducees, didn't like it so they arrested Peter and John and brought them into their court for questioning. It's a humorous story to me because I can just imagine the scene. The accusers are so angry, but they don't know what to say. They are furious, but it becomes extremely difficult for them to deny this man has been healed. After all, the man who was healed at Beautiful Gate, who was disabled and unable to walk from birth, was a man they would have frequently walked past on their way to the temple, and here he was now, standing, unafflicted, there beside them.

> But since they could see the man who had been healed standing there with them, there was nothing they could say.
>
> (Acts 4:14)

Acts 4:13 says that when the officials met Peter and John and heard their defence they came to two conclusions about them. This part is so powerful it makes me emotional. The two conclusions were these:

1. 'they were unschooled, ordinary men';
2. 'these men had been with Jesus'.

That's what it says; you can read it for yourself. They could see, more than anything else, that these men had been with Jesus. Despite their rough edges and visible limitations, these men had been frequently in the company of Jesus.

> When they saw the courage of Peter and John and realised that they were unschooled, ordinary men, they were astonished and they took note that these men had been with Jesus.(Acts 4:13)

## Body odour

I find it interesting that every family has their own smell. You can identify it when you go into someone's home, or you can smell it on their clothes. I don't understand the science behind it all but I find it fascinating. Apparently we each have a signature odour as unique as a fingerprint, and people in the same household, after a while, start to smell the same because of shared bacteria. To me, it's sort of similar to what the religious leaders were saying to Peter and John: 'You smell the same as Jesus.'

I read this story again recently in Acts and became moved deeply inside because it all started to make sense. On that mountain, detailed in Mark 3, Jesus set his friends' life course like a rocket thrusting towards outer space. He asked them on a mountainside, where no one else was present, to make being with him their radical root, the thing that mattered most to them. He made no false promises about what being with him would bring. In fact he assured them frequently that life would be hard, there would be much opposition and not everyone would like them, but that his original request would remain the same: 'Be with me, my friends.'

Being with Jesus was certainly a duty for the disciples and a sticker on their back which attracted much hate and ultimately, for many of them, death. But it was worth it to them. Being with Jesus became life itself, like oxygen to their lungs, the axis their motives and activity moved around. Even the apostle Paul, after he encountered Jesus on the road to Damascus, felt the same. He writes in Philippians 1:21:

> My true life is the Anointed One, and dying means gaining more of him. (TPT)

Helen H. Lemmel was a hymn writer, born in England in 1863, who wrote around 500 hymns in her lifetime. At the height of Helen's musical career in the United States she became blind. In 1918, her missionary friend gave her a tract entitled *Focused*. The pamphlet contained these words, which immediately gripped her heart: 'So then, turn your eyes upon him, look full into his face and you will know that the things of this earth will acquire a strange new dimness.' Shortly afterwards, Helen penned the famous hymn 'Heavenly Vision', which includes the words:

> Turn your eyes upon Jesus,
> Look full in His wonderful face,
> And the things of earth will grow strangely dim
> In the light of His glory and grace.

## Questions

- Have you responded to Jesus the rabbi's 'Follow me' request and chosen to make being with him your radical root?

- Write down any reflections you may have, considering that today, Jesus' greatest desire is for you to be with him.

_____
_____
_____
_____

# 7
# HIS SECRET CHAPTER

*The [person] who would truly know God must give time to Him.*
A. W. TOZER

God longs for us to know him. Jesus' apprentices discovered the way to know him was to be with him. I want to home in on some specifics surrounding knowing God and subsequently being with Jesus. As I previously stated, one of the greatest pleasures of this life is being intimately connected to God; I sense deep within it's what I was created for. All that is in God, the full expansive expression of his nature, is available to us. But deliberately seeking God alone, where no one is looking, has to be a part of our 'being with him'. This isn't my own intelligent theory; it's Jesus' teaching, which I hope this chapter will unpack more.

## Secret chapter

In Matthew 6, people are gathered around to listen to Jesus teach and he begins to share some of his 'secrets' that are worth noting. First, Jesus talks about the 'secret' of giving away money. He says, referring to the Pharisees:

> When you give to the needy, do not announce it with trumpets, as the hypocrites do in the synagogues and on the streets, to be honoured by others. Truly I tell you, they have received their reward in full. But when you give to the needy, do not let your left hand know what your right hand is doing, so that your giving may be in secret. Then your Father, who sees what is done in secret, will reward you.
>
> (Matthew 6:2–4)

Meaning in simple terms: If you give to those in need in order to be affirmed and acknowledged by others, you are not evil, but you will just receive a temporary, human reward when there is a heavenly one available.

Jesus goes on to reveal the way to pray, and it's the same advice:

> And when you pray, do not be like the hypocrites, for they love to pray standing in the synagogues and on the street corners to be seen by others. Truly I tell you, they have received their reward in full. But when you pray, go into your room, close the door and pray to your Father, who is unseen. Then your Father, who sees what is done in secret, will reward you.
>
> (Matthew 6:5–6)

It seems God holds a high value for sons and daughters who live secret lives with him. It's intriguing that Jesus is so willing to tell us we will receive a reward for something we do. God isn't a slot machine; we don't curry favour with him by doing religious practices so we can force his hand for our agenda. I believe wholeheartedly in the fundamental teaching that no human being can do enough to earn God's time or affection, as I spoke of in a previous chapter. But as we so often find in Scripture, a tension does exist, because Jesus is saying there *is* a reward from his Father for those who intentionally choose to pray in the way Jesus laid out.

Hebrews 11:6 says something similar: [God] rewards those who earnestly seek him.

He rewards those who seek him when no one else is looking. Don't get it confused, though; it's not a reward of riches, popularity or even a strategy for our next ministry endeavour. It is God himself. God is the reward and he is the best reward there is. There is something within God you cannot acquire anywhere else. The best teachers, worship music, ministry school or books can't give it to you. It's a reward that you have to go to God himself for. But those who move beyond weekly meetings and into a private, consistent, personal pursuit of God will, without question, position themselves to receive a reward from God. I've found the more I labour in this great pursuit, the more there is something in me that yearns for this intimate knowing of God that can only be truthfully sustained as I pursue this precious secret.

## Quality time

When I met Maria, it was clear we were very different. In fact, apart from speaking the same language occasionally, I wondered if we were opposite in every way possible. We argued a lot about spending time together when we first started dating. Maria would burst into tears, seemingly out of nowhere, and tell me through sobs, 'We never spend quality time together.' I would often try to say something sympathetic and understanding, but my face would not agree with my words. Maria would let me know fairly quickly that I didn't understand her and I would blurt out in frustration something like: 'We've been together so much this week! I've seen you almost every night.' That same conversation happened over and over again. It seems silly now that it took me so long to figure out what was really going on.

The problem, which I discovered much later, was that naively I thought time together was about just being in the same room as Maria, whether that was with my roommates or out at a party. What Maria slowly taught me about quality time is less about quantity and more about having each other's full attention when we are together, which is very hard to do unless you have periods when you are alone. My point is I think that what Jesus is saying in Matthew 6 isn't that we are supposed to become hermits and live in our rooms with the curtains drawn. I think Jesus is saying the same thing Maria told me: 'It's hard to feel connected when we are never alone together.'

Now we are married, Maria and I are together a lot throughout the week, but much of that time is spent doing normal stuff: we cook together, see friends and sometimes both work from home. But time can be deceptive. Similar to when we first met, that way of living can make us both assume we've had quality time together because we have been sharing the same air, but we haven't actually connected.

We have often experienced the repercussions of not spending intentional time together. I become frustrated about really petty things and rapidly become selfish, forgetting about Maria's needs. It's being together alone with each other's undivided attention which keeps us connected amidst the busyness of life. I can easily think I'm connected to God after I've been to church or hung out with another Christian, but really these activities are just a mirage, hiding us from the truth. True connection with the divine moves out from that place where we are alone, face to face with God.

I cannot deny the magnitude of what I met head on in my room all those years ago whilst I was working in that workshop doing my apprenticeship. Since finding God in my room, I've been left feeling short-changed by church. It's nothing against the gathering; I'm a pastor and believe that coming together frequently is an essential part of being part of his body. I just need something more to sustain me and I would argue that you probably do too. I'm jealous of the reward that God loves to impart in the secret place. The simple truth is it's *hard to be connected to God if we are never alone together.*

## Mountainside secrets

### TIP 1
*Being with Jesus must involve being alone with him.*

---

### Questions

- When was the last time you were intentionally alone with God?

Take a moment to think about the things that stop you from being alone with God.

_____
_____
_____
_____

## POEM

God would you move me to my own mountain
   I know the journey up there is a hard one
I've faced all kinds of thoughts
   And sometimes I feel like a fool to leave
But I am bankrupt without you
   So as the voices get more and more loud
Would you give me courage to leave the crowd and climb the mountain

     ('Take Me to the Mountain' by Timothypoet, featured on Prayers from the Mountain EP, 2020)

# 8

# CASH-MACHINE CHRISTIANITY

*You become what you behold.*
WILLIAM BLAKE

So a life of being with Jesus must involve being alone with him. Interestingly, Alexander Pope said: 'Blessed is the one who expects nothing, for he shall not to be disappointed.' It's an interesting thought, though I think the reality is we all bring expectations with us wherever we go, including our relationship with God. Personally, I think it's important to ask ourselves what we do expect to happen when we are alone with Jesus. Let me explain: there have been a few periods in my life when money was really tight. In those times, when you're living from pay cheque to pay cheque, it's a relief when you finally get paid. Sometimes at the end of the month when my wages had come through, I'd eagerly make a trip to the bank, put my card in the cash machine, look round, quickly shielding my pin number with my hand, and await the smooth notes handed out by the machine. If I'm really honest, spending time with God has often felt like going to the cash machine after getting paid, but for some reason, instead of money coming out, a sign comes up that says 'Declined' and I walk away frustrated with empty pockets. And as I'm walking away, positive I put all the digits in right, I question: what did I do wrong? I've thought that many times as I've sat in my room agitated and defeated after trying to connect with God. I'm not even totally sure what I expected to happen – just something. Maybe I need to pray differently or read more thoroughly. What did I miss? Something that has really helped me is this simple truth: *being is about becoming.*

From an early age in school we are taught that if a teacher asks a question and you get the right answer, that's good and you are doing well. Gold star. But when you get it wrong, or don't know the answer, you are bad and not doing well. Some of you may be thinking, *Well yes, Tim – what's your point, what's wrong with that?* My point is that slowly we can become conditioned to believe that we are doing well when we get the right results. So we ask our spiritual leaders or guides, the same way we asked our teachers at school: 'Just tell me what to do in my quiet time. Tell me how to be a good Christan and get good results.' We get panicky and full of condemnation when we feel we are not getting the 'right results', and conclude we must be doing something wrong.

If I may return to our road trip through America, I forgot to mention something that happened before we left Redding, California. Maria and I spent some time visiting the ministry school we had attended. I was going to sit in on the classes for the day but ended up talking with old friends outside the main auditorium. When I finally sat down anonymously at the back of the room, it was Bill Johnson talking (the senior leader of Bethel Church in Redding), and he said, in the way only Bill does, slowly and with great thought, 'I've written lots of books, and I will probably write more, but what I've realised is none of that will really matter when I get to Heaven. What will matter most when I get there is who I become while I'm here.'

When I heard that, I honestly immediately left the room, not because I was offended or bored but because something in me knew that was what I needed to be reminded of.

What matters in this life is who we are becoming. The apostle John said:

> Dear friends, we are already God's children, but he has not yet shown us what we will be like when Christ appears. But we do know that we will be like him, for we will see him as he really is.
>
> (1 John 3:2 NLT)

Do you catch what John is saying here? One day we will leave our bodies on earth; we will die and meet Jesus face to face in heaven and in that moment, when we first see him face to face, we will know with perfect vision who we are. We will become fully our originally designed self, undistorted in any way, in a blink of an eye. Why? Because seeing *him* clearly reveals *me* to me clearly. My transformation will be completed there once and for all – no more comparisons and second-guessing my identity. However, the process doesn't have to start there; it can start now. So we are invited on a journey of discovering more and more who God is and simultaneously being introduced to the person we were made to be. The more we are with Jesus, the clearer the picture gets. The more I come away from the busyness and the many demands of life and find God, the more I'm aware that the greatest and most significant process is taking place in me. Something is happening in the deepest part of who I am, whether I'm aware or not. I was made for this: to know and be known by God. Not in an observing 'oida' way but in an experiential 'ginosko' way, and the more I know him, the more I'm becoming the me I was always designed to be. Free from fear, comparisons and insecurity.

So, in my pursuit of God, I have to remind myself whenever I'm tempted in frustration to metaphorically smash the cash machine because it's given me 'no money', no quick results, that the most fulfilling outcome of being with Jesus isn't something I get from him instantaneously. Having said that, I very much relish it when it does happen and in a certain sense I deeply desire it – because I know some of the things he's revealed to me in an instant have come right when I needed it, like manna that fed me when I felt as if I was about to waste away inside. But that isn't what grounds me and keeps me showing up to the secret place. The ultimate success of my time with God isn't a revelation I can share with a friend or a sudden change in my emotions. Instead, it's something that is happening deep within me; it's who I'm slowly becoming in his presence.

◇◇◇◇◇◇◇◇◇◇◇◇◇◇

## Mountainside secrets

### TIP 2
The fruit of being with Jesus is who you are slowly becoming.

---

**Question ?**

Does knowing that intentionally being with God is most about who we are becoming change the way you might approach being with him?

_____
_____
_____
_____

## PRAYER FOR THOSE BECOMING

Heavenly Father, I trust you;
That you are doing things within me I cannot see,
That you are the maker of all things worth being made.
I receive your grace today to relinquish control and relax into being with you.

# 9

# LEAVE YOUR CAMERA IN THE CAR

*Life moves pretty fast. If you don't stop and look around once in a while, you could miss it.*
FROM THE MOVIE *FERRIS BUELLER'S DAY OFF*

Back to our west coast road trip. After we somewhat reluctantly left LA, we travelled for hours through the dry desert into Las Vegas. I saw nothing worth mentioning but cactus plants and dry vegetation for hundreds of miles. I felt I was on the set of one of the John Wayne movies that my dad used to watch. Then suddenly we arrived. Welcomed by bright neon lights and a plethora of signs to casinos. Maybe it's because I'm from a small city in the west of England called Bath which has architecture from the Roman era, but Vegas felt weird to me, almost as if all the buildings were temporary. I felt as though

I was in *The Truman Show* – in a city surrounded by a bubble detached from the real world. We spent a night there walking through the busy streets and staring up at tall buildings. We went into a gigantic casino with live performances, countless bars, slot machines and black-jack wheels as far as the eye could see, all in a Parisian design with a big Eiffel Tower smack in the middle, reaching up to the ceiling. We stayed in a hotel that was also a casino. In the morning we set off for Arizona and more importantly the Grand Canyon.

As I said, I'm from Bath, and not to show off (even though I will anyway) but Bath is a World Heritage Site, so I'm familiar with tourists. They wander aimlessly through the streets pointing at random buildings that seem insignificant to me, posing with their long selfie sticks. I guess everyone has a disdain for tourists in their own city. Obviously I understand because I'm the same when I go to places of natural beauty. I visited Niagara Falls with some of my friends on a trip to Canada. My heart raced as I heard the powerful roar of the crashing water a mile away as we found a car parking space. But I realised, slightly embarrassingly in retrospect, that when I was actually at the falls, I spent the whole time trying to get the perfect picture with the water in the background whilst avoiding the spray and resisting the pressure of other tourists wanting to move in and capture their own perfect photo, rather than just enjoying being there.

Well finally, at the Grand Canyon national park we arrived at our accommodation. It was bitterly cold as we left the car, snow covering the ground right up to the house, which was quite a contrast to LA. The stars were luring me up to witness their wonder, so I stared upwards and enjoyed the clear sky. We then gathered in the kitchen and planned the next day's excursions. I couldn't wait. The following morning, we left just after first light and a coffee, as agreed, and drove an hour to the canyon. I stared out of the window most of the way and tried to guess when we were close. At the gate there was no one taking fees to enter because there was a dispute within the US government.

On our trip to America I forgot my DSLR camera which Maria had bought me for Christmas. Leaving it behind wasn't a big deal until we parked up at the Grand Canyon. I had all but forgotten about it until we were pulling into the bay and I unclipped my seat belt. Remembering again made me sink a little inside. I'm embarrassed to admit this because it makes me feel so shallow and such a millennial but I honestly thought to myself, *It's almost pointless going if I don't have my camera to capture it.* I said something along those lines to Maria and she replied with contempt, dismissing it sharply. But as we all walked towards the edge of the canyon I completely forgot about my camera. I could see people at the railings ahead gasping and turning to loved ones in awe. It truly was spectacular, and soon I was glad that I didn't have my camera. I stood and looked without talking for a long time, holding on to the railing, looking around from different angles and staring way down to the bottom where I could see a bridge that crossed over the river. We walked around for hours – some of us thought for too long – looking from different points and gazing deep into the gorge.

## Gazing

I have a friend called Paul Wakely who I've been getting to know over the last few years. I've known him all my life but lately he's become like a father to me. Paul's in his seventies and has been a pastor in my city since before I was even born. He's the kind of person who gives you all their attention and has almost a magical power, even in one short exchange, to make you feel that God himself has seen right into you. Paul was talking to me on the phone the other day; he always speaks slowly with a loving tone that I imagine God himself shares and almost lulls me to a half-sleep. I had been thinking a lot about this whole pursuit of being with Jesus when I called him, and was intrigued to hear his views, so I asked, 'How do you spend time with Jesus?'

He replied, 'Oh Tim, I do a lot of gazing.'

At first I wasn't quite sure if he'd said 'grazing', not 'gazing', which would have been a very different response. I had never heard of 'gazing'. It sounded quite weird, but I was curious. Apparently that's what he calls it, but he openly admitted he stole the idea from Psalm 27:4:

> One thing I ask from the Lord,
>   this only do I seek:
> that I may dwell in the house of the Lord
>   all the days of my life,
> to gaze on the beauty of the Lord
>   and to seek him in his temple.

It's helpful to understand that this psalm was not written in David's comfortable armchair in his palace as he ruled triumphantly as king. Instead it was written in the early years of his life as he fled to mountains and caves, escaping from King Saul who wanted to kill him. The one thing David desired was to gaze on the Lord's beauty. Amazing. This was his quest before God as he hid in the shadows of mountains. Just one more look, one more gaze upon you, God.

Often in the past, when I have spent time alone with God, it's as if I have a notepad with a list of things I think I need to pray and achieve. Other times, I've come to him as though I'm preparing to listen to a Ted Talk, ready to write down a significant revelation I can take away and quote later. It's embarrassing to admit this but I do it all the time.

After Paul told me about gazing he added, still with softness and compassion in his voice, but a little concerned, 'Tim, don't bring anyone into the room with you when you are with Jesus.' He continued so gently it almost moved me to tears: 'Tim, God loves our company.' Then he mentioned a quote, but he couldn't remember where he'd read it. I scribbled the quote down almost illegibly on a piece of paper next to me as he continued to talk, eager not to miss anything.

After we'd finished speaking I put the phone down on my desk and sat in silence for several minutes. Then I started staring out of the window at the golf course way in the distance, just about making out someone taking a shot. After a while I looked down at my scrap of paper and just about made out the words I had written down in a hurry: *Behold the one that beholds you and smiles.*

I read it over and over again numerous times. I chewed on the truth that when God thinks of me he smiles, and I could feel a warm feeling stirring in my heart. Weirdly, as I sat there mulling it over, I was reminded of my trip to the Grand Canyon. I remembered how I'd forgotten my camera, but in the end how I enjoyed its wonder even more. *That's it*, I suddenly thought. *That's the answer!* The key to being with Jesus is to leave your camera in the car. I felt God sort of lean in, affirming that when I'm with him I should just enjoy being there, enjoy his beauty and bask in the wonder of who he is. I thought about reading all the plaques and information boards at the Grand Canyon. They had dates about when it was formed and maps showing how far it reached down. Even as I recalled that specific part of the memory, it was as if God was saying I don't need to understand it all when I'm with him. It's really great to just be there, to soak in the simple knowledge that God, the creator of every natural beauty, likes my company. *To behold the one that beholds me and smiles.* Enjoy being enjoyed by him and nothing else, no strings attached.

Sometimes I still 'take my camera to the canyon'. I come to God with my agendas and checklists, wanting something to show for my time. But God is kind; he reminds me again and again that what he really wants is for me to bravely leave it all behind and just be there.

I started practising gazing at Jesus the way I did standing at the railing of the canyon – appreciating him for who he is. A God who is. A God whom I ultimately can't control. It's normal after gazing at Jesus to feel nothing. I say that confidently because Paul warned me it would happen sometimes. But because I have this new filter – 'this is about who I am becoming' – I don't feel as anxious about that any more.

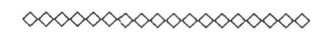

◇◇◇◇◇◇◇◇◇◇◇◇◇◇

## Mountainside secrets

### TIP 3
A great way to be with Jesus is to learn to behold him.

### Response

- Read the psalm below slowly a few times until you feel a settling and a slight movement towards the affection of Christ for you.

- Now try simply gazing upon God without speaking or praying. If you feel your mind wandering, it's OK. Return to the verse and allow yourself to be uncomfortable at the canyon without your camera.

Here's the one thing I crave from Yahweh,
the one thing I seek above all else:
I want to live with him every moment in his house,
beholding the marvelous beauty of Yahweh,
filled with awe, delighting in his glory and grace.

(Psalm 27:4 TPT)

# SECTION THREE
# The Approach

# 10

# SWIMMING THROUGH WHITE WATER

*If in doubt, paddle out.*
NAT YOUNG, WORLD SURFING CHAMPION 1966

Growing up in south-west England, I enjoyed going with my family at least once a year to the coast, usually Devon or Cornwall. Our favourite place was Polzeath in North Cornwall where we would camp for a week in a field over the road from the beach. The road was covered on either side by sand and people walked barefoot everywhere with no real sense of purpose or place to be. It was amazing. We each had something we could go off and do at the beach. I would find a private spot on the rocks in my own world, way out into the sea, and fish with a spinner for mackerel, gambling on a quick cast whilst trying to avoid the waves, retreating as they crashed in against the rocks.

James, my older brother, is an adrenalin junky. He does rock climbing these days and he's very talented, but back then, he was more into jumping off cliffs than climbing up them. He would search online for the best spots, then traipse us all to the cliff side to nervously watch him leap, making sure someone videoed him on his camera so he could use the footage for one of his summer edits.

Dad has a weird obsession with finding treasure (as he describes it, not me) caught in the rocks after high tide. He would spend hours and hours dislodging fishing tackle and buoys with a pen knife, then lug them back to the campsite. Once, when Dad was dragging his loot back to where we were sitting on the beach, we caught sight of him way in the distance carrying what looked like a large octopus. As he got closer we could see it was green. Steve blurted out 'What's Dad found now?!' and we all burst into laughter. Then we each started making wild speculations about what he might have found. When he finally got to us, we discovered he had found enough rope to tie a large ship to a dock. He dropped it proudly in front of us with a big grin. We all felt quite embarrassed. Mum told him, 'You're not taking that home,' but Dad argued that it would come in very useful. There wasn't enough space in the car so he attached it to the roof; it covered the whole top of the car from the front to the back. We all hid our faces as we left the car park, trying to avoid eye contact with the cool surfers.

Hannah, my younger sister, would dart back and forth, in and out of the sea. Bodyboarding for a while, then running back to the beach with blue hands as she was so cold. I can picture her now, smiling avidly but shivering profusely with a large towel draped over her.

Most days, Mum would try to wake us up early and march us off for long walks along the coast until we moaned enough for her to let us turn back. She exclaims every holiday how much she loves the beach and teases us about moving down to Polzeath one day.

However, it's Steve who really loves the beach. He's a proper surfer. He bought a thick winter wetsuit one year with a hood he could pull over his head. Surfing is enjoyable for any novice satisfied with riding broken waves into the shore. Everyone has a go, from young children who can barely walk, to old grandparents. But surfing is hard work if you want to ride waves the way you see it on TV. Not to mention the standing-up-on-the-board part! Just getting to a position where you can stand on the board is incredibly arduous.

Steve always wanted to be out there with the real surfers – beyond the messy white water and inexperienced bodyboarders. Past the broken waves, there is a calm and tranquillity as you wait for the big waves to come in. Steve would talk about it as though it was the greatest feeling in the world, being out there sitting on his board in this wide-open space just looking cool. We would all go into the water together after helping each other squeeze into our skin-tight wetsuits. I remember once Steve peeing in his wetsuit as we were all waist deep wading out; he tried to convince us it's what all the real surfers do to keep warm.

As we moved out further, Steve would inevitably try to encourage us to swim out to the big waves where our toes could no longer touch the seabed. But after a short time of being battered and dragged underwater by the crashing waves I would get cold and frustrated and head back to the beach. Steve, however, would be out there for hours battling the waves. He would finally appear from the water, his board tucked under his arm, running out of the sea as if he was in *Baywatch*. When he got to our base on the beach, he would be eager to ask us if we had seen him catch a specific wave and then, before we could answer, explain moment by moment what happened.

What I've come to discover about my pursuit of God is that it's much the same as surfing. Let me explain. There is a space I know I was born to occupy frequently, the place I've spent much of this book talking about. It's a lonely, yet open place, where I discover Jesus and in turn get introduced increasingly to the true me. I've come to realise that space, just like the calm waters that light up Steve's face, is where my heart longs to be more than anywhere else. But similar to Steve when he's surfing, I first have to swim through my own violent white water and crashing waves. I've come to acknowledge the only way out there is through great resistance.

Some beaches we have visited, such as Putsborough in North Devon, have incredible surf, so occasionally there would be competitions with professional surfers. I remember us all as a family sitting together on the grass overlooking the sea, watching them with our achy muscles, salty hair and sun-kissed cheeks. I felt like a surfer even though I knew I wasn't one, staring out to the sea, picturing myself hours earlier gasping for air under a wave, momentarily poking my head up like a seal above the water and gazing out to where I wanted to be with little hope. Often in competitions the organisers have jet skis that they use to transport the surfers out to the big waves, past the white water. I remember thinking that was so unfair, that they avoided all the gruelling work fighting to get out there.

You know, often I've thought that that is what it's like for other people in their pursuit of God, especially some preachers I've heard. That they must know something I don't, because they are always, effortlessly, out in the deep with God. I heard the American evangelist Todd White talk a while ago and he said he had been praying for three hours that morning before he came to speak to us. I can't remember much of what he said after that; I was too distracted thinking about how someone could pray for that amount of time. It felt so hopelessly unattainable to me, similar to those huge waves that can tower over you.

What I've discovered recently after talking to preachers and pastors, and now being one myself, is that everyone experiences resistance in their pursuit of God. Yes, some don't like to admit it, but everyone does. No one gets jet ski privileges. We are all faced with two options: either swim through the waves or go back to the shore. And that is quite sobering. Truthfully it seems that rarely do we find God by accident. Hebrews 11:6 speaks to just that:

> [God] rewards those who sincerely seek him.
>
> (NLT)

My regular experience was that the moment I was getting ready to spend time alone with God, my mind was on everything else but God. I felt consumed with all kinds of thoughts: tasks for that day, people I should call, what to eat for dinner. I wasn't conscious of all these things at the time; I just knew that whenever I thought about being alone with God, there was an undeniable resistance that appeared, like the disheartening sight of another wave moving relentlessly towards me.

Steven Pressfield in his iconic book *The War of Art* makes it very clear that resistance is often an indicator you are focusing attention in places that matter most to who you are. For a long time that resistance caused me to live in a repetitive cycle of heading back to the shore, waiting for a day when the waves would die down and it would be easier to get out into the deep water. But it seems that the waves never die down. There is never a clear day that feels like the perfect conditions to meet God. So it seemed as if I could never quite get there, never quite push past the white water into that open space I had heard about so often.

What I have concluded in my own pursuit of God (and this may be an obvious statement) is that there is an enemy and he doesn't present himself like the devil with a red face and horns, the way he's drawn in pictures. But if everything we need is found beyond those waves, if God really does reward those who stay in the water like Steve and seek him, then our enemy has to be cunning to keep us outside this sacred area. So he uses all his best tricks to keep us on the shore.

I used to get so frustrated when I was younger because I would read book after book about the presence of God and subsequently grow in passion for a deeper relationship with him, but I never actually knew how to push through and get there. I would see people who seemed to spend days on end beyond the waves in glorious delight with God, but I struggled to even sit still for ten minutes. The following short chapters by no means hold all the answers. We each must find our own way and face our own waves, but I do hope they provide some practical insight into what has helped me to keep swimming into the deep.

> Resistance is experienced as fear; the degree of fear equates to the strength of Resistance. Therefore the more fear we feel about a specific enterprise, the more certain we can be that that enterprise is important to us and to the growth of our soul. That's why we feel so much Resistance. If it meant nothing to us, there'd be no Resistance.
>
> (Steven Pressfield, *The War of Art: Winning the Inner Creative Battle*)

# 11

# LEARNING TO LIVE DETHRONED

*In the beginning you were led into his presence by prayer; but now as prayer continues, the prayer actually becomes his presence ... You begin to discover that God is more intimately present to you than you are to yourself, and a great awareness of the Lord begins to come to you.*

JEANNE GUYON

God is not a God of disorder but of peace.

(1 Corinthians 14:33)

The world started in darkness and then God created. But chaos is still present, upturning lives and pulling families apart. I know that to be true, not just because of everything I see around me but often because of what I feel within me. But God brings order, not resembling a power-tripped boss, but by bringing his peace-filled 'shalom' order.

A. W. Tozer writes in his book *Knowledge of the Holy: The Attributes of God*:

Sin has many manifestations but its essence is one. A moral being, created to worship before the throne of God, sits on the throne of his own selfhood and from that elevated position declares, 'I AM.'

We all want to to live with peace, but it seems peace that comes from God begins through our surrender. Tozer goes on to paint a fascinating picture of what takes place when a human decides to make Jesus Lord of their lives and find true definition in Christ. In the picture there are steps that reach up to a throne, but the throne is empty. Then we see a human brush past Jesus, shoulder to shoulder, as the human steps down and Jesus steps up, Jesus willingly taking his seat on the throne. When Jesus is firmly placed on the throne of our own selfhood, we live in his order. But he will not strong-arm us for the seat; he is not a tyrant dictator. We can easily put ourselves, other people, items or idols back onto the throne – and we do this often! We must affirm, reinstate and celebrate Jesus' rightful position as often as possible, dealing with seat-hoggers like ego and worship of people. When Jesus is on the throne of our hearts he governs us with peace, causing us to continually become better vessels of the divine.

Mark's Gospel tells us that one day Jesus met a rich man who was trying hard to follow God by keeping all the Jewish commandments:

> Looking at the man, Jesus felt genuine love for him. 'There is still one thing you haven't done,' he told him. 'Go and sell

all your possessions and give the money to the poor, and you will have treasure in heaven. Then come, follow me.' At this the man's face fell, and he went away sad, for he had many possessions.

(Mark 10:21–22 NLT)

Jesus wasn't interested in the rich man's coins – he didn't need them for his cause. It wasn't even about the poor. Jesus just wanted to see if the man would dethrone the little god he had allowed to occupy the seat meant for Jesus. He was longing to be the ultimate winner of his heart.

I'm convinced wholehearted surrender must become the constant rhythm for any person who longs for God's peace and order to move through their lives. Bravely stepping off the throne where we have taken it back, giving Jesus space to sit and be God in our lives, is how we return to the true essence of our humanity.

## Mountainside secrets

### TIP 4
Approach God's presence through wholehearted surrender.

## POEM

Highest praises, empty stages,
glory filling basements and forgotten places.
The presence of Jesus sweeping across the nations,
from hustling workstations to places that can't be named here.
We are being awakened to the good news,
God is on the move.
Not in an institution or a group,
but in hearts that have turned into homes.
Homes where he can be enthroned.
A throne that isn't my own is now the most Holy's clothed in bones.

('Highest Praises' by Timothypoet)

## PRAYER FOR THOSE GIVING JESUS BACK THE THRONE

Jesus, I surrender. Be Lord again in my life. Help me to let go of control so you sit on the throne of my heart. Have dominion over my thoughts; reign over my body and emotions. I want my whole being to bend low and make way for the King of Kings. You are the worthy one, my all in all. So with an open and honest heart I give you permission to remove the seat-hoggers, the idols and little gods, and take your place again at the centre of my world, on the throne.

# 12
# WRESTLING WITH GOD

I sat on my favourite bench next to the canal
And I heard you say that you were pleased
I felt you plead with me not to leave
So I chose to stay and bathed in that uncomfortability
Not knowing what to say
Yet knowing that that was OK
I felt myself slowly sink like a ship into your sea
And you exposed the busy bee
So distracted it couldn't see
How infatuated you are with me
Your pleasure began confronting all that I thought was important
Not to correct but to give me rest
Because I was such a mess trying to meet everyone's needs.

(From 'The Canal' by Timothypoet,
featured on *Prayers from the Mountain* EP, 2020)

Can I be honest? 'Pursuing God' rarely looks the way I think it will. Typically, 'seeking his face', as David puts it, requires me to let go of self somewhere in the process. Maybe that's why it takes time – because I don't often want to release my grip on self. We talked about it briefly in the previous chapter but I think it's worth unpacking more. Each Gospel writer quotes these words from Jesus in their account: 'For whoever would save his life will lose it, but whoever loses his life for my sake will find it.' Maybe thats why so many of the Mothers and Fathers of the Christian faith talked about 'forgetting oneself'. From Jeanne Gunyon in the sixteenth century who said, 'We must forget *ourselves*, and all self-interest, and listen and be attentive to God.' To A.W. Tozer who wrote similarly 400 years later in the 1940s, 'Forgive me for thinking of myself. Help me to forget myself and find my true peace in beholding Thee.'

## Our true self

I'm not convinced we must deny all self, in the sense that we are left as Jesus-clones, void of any personality. The apostle Paul says, 'It is no longer I who live, but Christ who lives in me' (Galatians 2:20 ESV). In essence, Paul is suggesting that our truest self is wrapped up in Christ. The most defining part of him is Christ's inner-dwelling. If we let him, Jesus will weave into us, infusing into our personhood, transforming us into a new kind of human. But 'Christ in us' does not mean we are hollowed out, with all our quirks and interests discarded, left a shell that Jesus can occupy. Forgetting oneself is essential on this journey, but I believe it's about dissociating completely from the idea that any part of us can settle into its original design outside Christ.

We are obsessed with catering to the needs of false self in the modern age. I'm not opposed in large part to much of the 'self-help' content – it's helpful! But the honest truth is there is only so much other people can do to help you heal and unlock your true or best self. Ultimately, every person is aimlessly wandering through a foreign, unfamiliar land without a compass or map. All selfhood finds its authentic definition in Jesus and in Jesus alone.

I say this because I think it's important in what I am about to say next. I enjoy walking when I really want to connect with Jesus. There's a canal in Bath two minutes from where I live; I wander along it at a painfully slow pace. Often at first, my walk is filled with wrestling. That's what I have come to call it anyway. It's as if I'm internally rolling around, similar to fighters on a mat, wrestling with accusing thoughts like: *What are you doing out here? God doesn't want to speak to you! This is not a productive use of time!* Then frustration usually mounts, which adds to the wrestle as I become disappointed with the fact that I'm spending time and energy 'wrestling' and not 'connecting with God'. But slowly, as I continue to walk and wrestle, something seems to happen in me. My soul begins to slowly surrender control, sometimes in places I didn't even realise I was holding on. It's as if my selfhood begins to kneel in humility again. It's as if I realise again on a heart level that there is truly no answer within myself. I walk more and begin to tell God that fact in different ways as I come to terms with this exquisite yet simple truth: God is not my possession. I can't convince him to agree to any of my terms. In this process my heart relinquishes some of its tightness and opens up; I begin to acknowledge him for who he really is. And he guides me gently to a more open place where my whole personhood is again securely in the hands of God.

I guess what I'm trying to say is: If you feel as though you're wrestling, don't give up. There's a blessing coming at daybreak, just as there was for Jacob who wrestled with God:

> Then the man said, 'Your name will no longer be Jacob, but Israel, because you have struggled with God and with humans and have overcome.'
> Jacob said, 'Please tell me your name.'
> But he replied, 'Why do you ask my name?' Then he blessed him there.
>
> (Genesis 32:28–29)

## Mountainside secrets

### TIP 5
We can approach God through surrender by wrestling.

# A PRAYER FROM A HUNGRY HEART

Lord, I am hungry. Take me out of yesterday and tomorrow and place my feet firmly here, today. I can't live off the taste of yesterday's food. I need the bread of life to fill me again. I've tasted and I've seen and now my stomach is grumbling, reminding me it's daily bread, not one meal rationed for the week. So I invite you to fill me. Nourish me like a plant that has its roots extended as far as it can reach. I know I'm not myself when I haven't eaten, so here I am again sitting at your table. Teach me to feast, to enjoy you, to delight in being delighted in. You are the food that fills. So give me today my daily bread.

# 13

# DISARMED

Be still, and know that I am God.

(Psalm 46:10)

I've read Psalm 46 countless times. People write it on wooden signs and stick it on their fridges. It's the motto for slow slips of morning coffee, and rightly so, but I will never forget when I read it on my honeymoon, sitting by the pool in the villa Maria and I were staying in. Wedged in a beanbag absorbing the warm Greek sun with my Bible open on this psalm, I heard God whisper into my thoughts plainly as I recited this familiar verse: 'Tim, there is no true knowing of me apart from stillness.' I lay there for a long while listening to the gentle lapping of the water in the pool, just mulling it over. I felt even more relaxed, as if I might sink deeper into the beanbag to a place of no return. I kept repeating that phrase in my head. I wanted to say I'd got it; possibly I did on a certain level, but not completely.

Back at home, that thought kept returning to me, cycling through my mind, and I was never totally sure where it was leading me to. 'There is no true knowing of God apart from stillness.'

I began digging and found out that the words 'Be still' in this verse are from the Hebrew root word *raphah*, which has a wide variety of meanings, but in its truest sense it means to slacken or let go. For example:

> He pours contempt on nobles
> and disarms the mighty. (Job 12:21)

The word 'disarms' here is *raphah*.

The word is used 46 times in the Scriptures; in one place it means 'to draw into the evening' and in another 'to sink down'. When David writes, 'Be still, and know that I am God,' he is using a word that speaks of being weak or letting go, like a taut rope holding a ship to a port that's finally able to loosen. It's not just sitting without body movement but yielding your soul or coming to the end of yourself.

I'm convinced more than ever that 'being still', disarmed and feeble before the Lord, is a powerful key to help us begin to truly know him.

## *Mountainside secrets*

### TIP 6
Practise surrender by the way of stillness.

## PRACTISING BEING STILL (TAKES FIVE MINUTES)

1. Start by closing your eyes and taking a few deep breaths. Imagine you are sitting on your own beanbag beside a pool. You can pick the country. The sun is warming your whole body. You can hear the sounds of the pool and birds in the distance.
2. Now imagine yourself sinking more and more into the beanbag …
3. The more you physically sink, picture yourself becoming less and less yours and more and more his, surrendering to God's presence.
4. Take a moment to reflect on this experience, recording any thoughts or feelings.

# 14
# OPENINGS EVERYWHERE

Scripturally, as early as the book of Exodus, we see a priest defined as an official who was set apart from the rest of the community to carry out duties associated with worship and sacrifices. 'Ministers of the Lord' (see Joel 1:9) functioned as mediators of God's presence and were responsible for the day-to-day operation of the tabernacle and eventually the temple in Jerusalem. It's fascinating as an exercise to read Exodus–Leviticus at the same time as Hebrews and see the extent of God's overarching purpose in his Son Jesus relating to the position of the priest.

> Day after day every priest stands and performs his religious duties; again and again he offers the same sacrifices, which can never take away sins.
>
> (Hebrews 10:11)

Priests, as well as high priests, practised daily duties for the Lord in the Holy Place, which was within the temple. These duties included lighting the candles, topping up incense and offering up prayers on behalf of the people. But once a year, after a series of cleansing rituals, the high priest could go alone to the most restricted place on earth. Through the thick curtain that divided the outer courts from the Most Holy Place. It was holy because Yahweh, the Holy One, was present there. So once a year the high priest lingered in the tabernacle, present with God himself, just as Moses and Joshua had done in the desert. Not because they were obliged to, but because it was their reward, their prize and perk for all their faithful duty. But when Jesus died, it was the beginning of a whole new way:

> When Jesus had cried out again in a loud voice, he gave up his spirit. At that moment the curtain of the temple was torn in two from top to bottom. The earth shook, the rocks split ...
>
> (Matthew 27:50–51)

The writer of Hebrews explains even further the drastic significance of that moment when Jesus died and simultaneously the curtain, which was in place to separate people from God's presence, was torn:

> ... sacrifice for sin is no longer necessary. Therefore, brothers and sisters, ... we have confidence to enter the Most Holy Place by the blood of Jesus, by a new and living way opened for us through the curtain, that is, his body.
>
> (Hebrews 10:18–20)

I don't want my heart to be numbed to the weighty reality of this statement. Not only is 'sacrifice for sin no longer necessary' but also we should 'have confidence to enter the Most Holy Place' because Jesus' broken and beaten body is our way in. The great divide has been destroyed from top to bottom, the curtain was torn, and now there is a new and living way in! Now Jesus is the great high priest standing at the entrance welcoming us in and the curtain is open everywhere. The door to his presence is ajar in every country and community, and no matter how hateful my thoughts or lacklustre my day's performance, the door is open. The door is open!

Clearly the open door is not in old Jerusalem at the physical temple. We don't have to travel to Israel to enter the Lord's presence. But now by the Spirit we can enter his presence anywhere. Openings are available to everyone, all the time, but it seems at certain moments I'm personally more aware of them. And the more I accept their invitation with reverence and expectation like the high priests and move through them, the more openings I seem to stumble across. Not just in my private prayer time but also on the building site or while walking to the supermarket. The writer of the book of Hebrews says that God 'rewards those who earnestly seek him' (Hebrews 11:6); God just asks us to make the first move. Seeking doesn't have to be dramatic like boldly migrating across land and sea. He rewards even the slightest movement in his direction. Even a simple thought directed his way when we're at work, for example, is enough to lead us through the open door that's been left ajar. It's not just open for the high priest, or for pastors or preachers. It's for bricklayers and nurses, mums and lorry drivers. It's open for normal people like me and you. If we would just turn towards him in even a small way, we would start to live more and more beyond the curtain where God is.

A personal hero of mine is Nicholas Herman, widely known as Brother Lawrence. I've read his short book, *The Practice of the Presence*, so much it is stained and tattered across all the edges. Brother Lawrence was a Frenchman who lived in a monastery in Paris in the 1600s. Lawrence's main job at the monastery was washing dishes, which freed him to practise his real passion: having constant fellowship with God.

His message was simple: think of God often. Just think of him. The writer of Hebrews says, 'Fix your thoughts on Jesus' (Hebrews 3:1). Our minds so easily become occupied with the things we need to do and the wants and desires of life. But what if we deliberately occupied our thinking with Jesus and his thoughts towards us? I wonder how the landscape would begin to change around a person who mastered the art of thinking about Jesus. I know that for Brother Lawrence, it changed everything. Kings and queens and powerful leaders journeyed to Brother Lawrence at the monastery high in the hills of France. It wasn't because he had any special talent or leadership quality, but simply because he had learnt to practise the presence. I imagine that they peered in through the window of his kitchen and gleaned anything they could from him whilst he washed the dishes.

Sometimes, my head feels like the Milky Way – thoughts spinning around like planets and stars zooming uncontrollably in all directions. But when my thoughts drift to Jesus and his loving place in my life, it's as if heaven is tangibly inviting me deeper, beyond the chaos of my own mind and into his delight.

> You tell me that I always say the same thing. What can I say? It is true. I don't know any easier method, nor do I practice any other, so I advise this one to everybody. We have to know someone before we can truly love him. In order to know God, we must think of Him often. Once we get to know Him, we will think about Him even more often, because where our treasure is, there also is our heart!
>
> (Brother Lawrence)

## Mountainside secrets

### TIP 7
Approach God with the mentality that there is always an open door to his presence.

## Question

Ask the Holy Spirit how you could grow in a day-to-day consciousness of the open door to his presence. Write down anything you think or feel.

_____
_____
_____
_____

# SECTION FOUR
# Practical Pointers

# 15

# A PRIVATE PURSUIT

I have to be perfectly honest: I am resistant to getting so practical about this topic. I feel poetic about it; I love the mystery and wonder that exists in communion with God. I'm afraid I will linearise or reduce this quest to a certain formula. I will, however, proceed with a few disclaimers, purely because I'm convinced it's critical to actually implementing and taking hold of this secret tangibly.

I believe God is in all things. From the silky sway of the trees I can see right now out of my window, to the inevitable conversation I'll have with the cashier shortly when I buy a sandwich for lunch at the supermarket. God isn't waiting for me when I get home from work as if he's an excited puppy at the door.

He isn't afraid of the 'real world' or the guys I work with on building sites. He longs for me to find him everywhere, in all things, mundane and monumentous. He's always been the God who delights in interrupting and influencing our every waking moment with his presence. Causing me to pause and appreciate, find beauty in pain, and consider his heart and approach to the people I encounter throughout my day. I want communion, a day-to-day and hour-by-hour type of connection. I'm positive that sustained connection (if I can call it that) flows from the 'alone space' I've been talking about.

A key element in any thriving marriage, as I've mentioned before, is for the spouses to have a flourishing private pursuit of each other. By 'private pursuit', what I don't mean is me posting on Instagram that I love Maria, or announcing it to a room full of people at church, though neither of these is wrong. But the real, honest health of our marriage is held up by consistently creating space to be alone together. When we are alone together for long enough, the things just below the surface show their head. Frustrations and disappointments appear, but also a desire to be known and understood by each other more deeply begins to find new passion. Relationships are beautifully fragile in that way. If Maria and I neglect that space, our marriage will not necessarily crash and burn, but inevitably we will drift apart even if we stay under the same roof. It's simply no different with God.

The chapters that follow are poised directly to help create that alone space in practical ways. I'm convinced that if we can develop a passionate quiet time, secret place, devotional time or any other term you choose to use, we will begin to really know God.

# 16

# WHEN AND WHERE

**Mad Hatter:** *(grabs Time's hand) I have time on my hand!*
**Time:** *(losing patience) You silly nitwits really think that I've not heard these cheap jabs before? Your attempts at mockery fall flat.*
**Mad Hatter:** *(plays with Time's shoulder pads) Look! Time is flying!*
**Time:** *(stands up furiously) Enough! No more wasting me!*
FROM THE MOVIE *ALICE THROUGH THE LOOKING GLASS*

Since discovering a simple tool a couple of years ago from Bob Sorge, it has become one of the greatest practical pieces of advice I've implemented into my life. I call this tool 'when and where'. When people ask me how I actually begin to develop a deeper devotional life with God, I usually start here. This basic practice for a person wanting to be with Jesus is as crucial as the blocks for a sprinter in a 100-metre race. Without them, you will find it hard to start. It's as simple as that.

Growing up going to church with my family, I grew accustomed to being around large numbers of people every week whom I knew on some vague level. I didn't know many of them well – I couldn't tell you when any of their birthdays were or any of the names of their children – but when I spoke to or interacted with many people in church I think an outsider looking in would have presumed we were all close friends. The thing is, the church I'm a part of, Life Church Bath, is filled with many kind and gifted people that I want to get to know better. So often, as I'm chatting to people before the service starts, I catch myself pointing at them across an aisle and saying, 'We should get together soon.'

But what I've realised over the years is this: until we actually put a time and place in our calendars, I don't have any confidence or expectation that 'getting together soon' will happen.

We can keep smiling and saying to each other every week before church, 'We really need to catch up,' and the next week laugh and say, 'Seriously, let's make it happen.' But until the conversation goes to 'When are you free this week?' and 'Where would be a convenient place to meet?', I know deep down, even if I wouldn't like to admit it, that it's just wishful thinking. That I'm not that committed to making it happen. Until we have decided *when and where*, spending time with someone is simply a fantasy, and we both know it. However, the moment we create a plan, we move out of fantasy and into a real and costly development of relationship with each other.

## Redeeming discipline

The same applies to developing a connection with God: unless I make a plan it's just a fantasy and always will be. Let's be perfectly clear, my plan will probably be very different from yours, but I've noticed that we often resist even having one. I find this intriguing. I accepted that without some discipline, I wouldn't be able to get fit enough to physically run the half marathon I signed up for. When I was in school, I wasn't naturally as bright as some of the other kids and it frustrated me how they could waltz into the exam hall professing how little revision they had done and still come out with grade 'A's. I knew, for me, that without some level of discipline to make me study (as hard as it was), I wouldn't do well in my exams.

Previously, in my head it always felt too structured and too religious to create a disciplined time and place with God, almost as if I was booking an appointment at the dentist. Maybe it's because I twitch slightly when I start detecting any sign of 'You must do this to be a good Christian', because I've seen how damaging that has been to me in the past.

## Dating Maria

What helped me change my mind about discipline was my relationship with Maria. We first met and started dating in Redding, California. It was a whirlwind of good and challenging emotion. Maria was ready for a serious relationship, but I wasn't. That's another story though. But one thing is for sure, as we got to know each other, I didn't have to try to pursue her.

I wrote her poems and she sent me postcards from different places she'd visited throughout the time we dated. I've got a whole stack of them that I keep under our bed.

About eight months into us going out, our relationship became long-distance. Maria began studying law at Bristol University in England and I stayed in the US, interning for a youth pastor named Tom Crandall. About six months into our time apart, Maria flew out to see me. We visited all our favourite places, including a town called Chico with quirky shops that Maria coos over. The next day we went for a Buddha bowl at a restaurant known as Wilda's; their Buddha bowls were famous in Redding (it's a very small city) and Maria had never tried one in the two years she had lived there.

With our bowls we drove to Whiskeytown to see the sunset. Whiskeytown is surrounded by snow-topped blue mountains, so tall that drifts of snow remain there almost year-round, even when Redding reaches its blistering 40°C summer temperatures. The lake is ice clear and the trees hang over the edge of the bank around the water. During that year, my housemates and I found a 'secret spot' away from the busier beaches, a narrow path winding down through the trees to a small, secluded stretch of beach. One of my housemates, Josiah, started taking other people there, which we told him was unacceptable. I had been arranging to propose to Maria there for weeks.

After we arrived at Whiskeytown with our Buddha bowls, we pulled up by the side of the road at the entrance to the secret spot. Maria was oblivious. At the time, I was convinced my cover had been blown because I saw a white car belonging to Robyn (Maria's best friend) parked up ahead in a lay-by, and I was sure Maria would recognise it. Maria wanted to sit in the car and finish her Buddha bowl, but I told her we would miss the sunset. She was annoyed, complaining that she'd be cold sitting and eating outside, but thankfully she complied.

It felt perfect. The sun was going down so I hurried Maria along as best I could, trying not to raise suspicion. I led the way, walking nervously down in between the trees, turning my feet to the side, trying not to slide too fast. I tried to hide my shaky hands as we arrived at the bottom, making our way through an opening of trees to the beach. Maria saw the lights and the blankets I had set up with Robyn previously and her momentary frustration turned to joy. My cold hands shook as I found the velvet box in my pocket and got down on one knee in front of her. We kissed and I tried to find words through tears as I stared at the ring, not quite believing I had just asked someone to marry me.

## Moving beyond fantasy

Six months later our lives had completely changed. We were married and living in the UK. I had started a new job as a youth pastor at Life Church, Maria was still doing her degree, but now we had moved into this old house, in the middle of nowhere, that we were going to renovate. Life quickly got full, but honestly not in a bad way. In fact there was so much good happening – dreams coming true and dreams being birthed. But then amongst it all, I started to acknowledge that my pursuit of Maria wasn't really happening.

I had a lot of weird ideas about relationships before I met Maria. Those three hours covering the time I proposed could have been in a movie, I reckon, but honestly the rest of the time it had felt very un-movie-like. I felt ashamed of my lack of desire for Maria; movies made me think we should be driven by a continual overwhelming passion for each other. But anyone who has been married for even a short time can attest that is not the case. I realised about a year into marriage that if I wanted to keep experiencing the joy and fruit that comes from our connection, something had to change. I had to move beyond fantasy and into a disciplined pursuit of Maria. I started writing reminders on my phone: 'Pursue Maria', and blocking out weekends in my diary to go away together. That's not to say our marriage lacks passion, absolutely not. It also doesn't lack spontaneous, unplanned pursuit. But now, having discipline doesn't make me feel bored and rigid – it makes me committed and really present in a relationship with a real person. I've moved beyond childish fantasy into a real lifelong pursuit of a person.

So now I see discipline with God differently too. I'm not in love with discipline but I *am* in love with God and I've found discipline is a necessary for a long-term lover. I can't expect being with God to just happen, hoping I'll find some time in my day. I've been there before, ignorantly, with the wool over my eyes. That's fantasy thinking. It may work for a couple of weeks, like when we first set eyes on someone we fancy.

But every person, at some point, must soberly ask themselves *when and where*. 'Let's get together sometime' will never cut it.

Even Jesus had to be brutally deliberate and disciplined about making space in his day to be with his Father. Even if we are in a less demanding season of life where we feel pursuit of God will happen more naturally. Don't believe the lie! We need to have a plan, or else the demands and distractions of life will strangle this beautiful gift. In Matthew 6, when teaching about where to pray, Jesus says very specifically, 'Go into your room and shut the door.'

Whether this is your first time thinking about asking this question or you've returned here, that's more than OK. This is always a good place to start and restart. I encourage you: take some time to think and respond to the questions below. *There are no right and wrong answers, but remember: be specific.*

## Questions

- When in the day would be a good time for you to be alone with God?

- Don't just write 'in the morning' or 'in the evening'. Be specific: what exact time? Is this my best time of the day? If not, maybe reconsider your time.

- Where could I do this? Again write the exact spot, for example 'on my favourite chair in the living room'.

_____
_____
_____
_____

◇◇◇◇◇◇◇◇◇◇◇◇◇◇◇

*Mountainside secrets*

### TIP
Decide when and where you will be alone with Jesus.

## PRAYER FOR THOSE DECIDING 'WHEN AND WHERE'

God, I want to know you, not just things about you. I want to be your friend, not just an acquaintance. I want to know you and be known by you, and I can see it will not happen by accident. I choose today to no longer be passive about our time together. I want to move beyond fantasy into the uncomfortable, costly reality of being with you. So I give this plan, this time and place to you, and pray you would bless it. I pray you would help me to be kind to myself when I fail and give me courage to be deliberate about meeting you alone again.

# 17

# PSYCHE OF A GARDENER

*Our devotional life with God is more like the planting of a garden. When we arise from sowing into the secret place, we will not usually be able to point to immediate results or benefits.*

BOB SORGE, *SECRETS OF THE SECRET PLACE*

My Dad is a simple man. He never wants presents for Christmas and, more than anything, he enjoys being outside with his hands in the soil. My mum bought my dad a smartphone a couple of years ago and he hates it. He told me he turns it off on purpose so no one can call him. If I want to get through to Dad, the best chance I have is to predict where he is and call someone who is with him. All he has ever known is physical work outside in the sun and rain with plants and animals. He grew up working on the family farm in England, then travelled to New Zealand, Canada and Germany doing different types of agriculture. For the last 30 years, since he got married to my mum, he has been a gardener.

In the first house renovation Maria and I did, the transformation wasn't only to the house but also the garden. I wish you could see photos of the garden. It was a total mess, overgrown and cluttered with piles of wood, paint pots and other random things old George had collected. Dad helped me completely change the area. I lost count of how many bonfires we had as we burned trees, bushes and old sheds. Working with Dad, I slowly realised how different our thinking was. As the area started to look more tidy I told Dad I wanted to grow plants that would make the garden look good for the summer and help us sell the house.

But as things started to take shape and we mapped out what we should grow, it became apparent that Dad wasn't even thinking about the summer coming. Dad wanted to plant things that would grow into the space and make the garden look spectacular for someone in ten years. He proudly planted four little yew trees in the border at the entrance to the house, and I stood and stared at them thinking, *Is that it?*

Dad looked at me and told me with a smile, 'They'll grow a foot a year if you're lucky,' as if they were some sort of super-tree.

I did the maths in my head, looking up past the trees, trying to see how many years it would be until they filled the space we'd planted them in.

At the front entrance of the house we had a massive drive that became thick mud most of the year. Everyone who came to see us grew to despise it, tiptoeing around puddles to get to the front door. I cringe and still feel bad for what we put our faithful postman through, enduring our drive every day. One morning I looked out of the window and saw him clinging onto a handful of letters and parcels and hopping like a gazelle over a 3-foot trench in the garden that we'd dug. Needless to say, everyone was over the moon when we began work on the driveway. We hired a mechanical digger and dug it up, creating some drainage for the excess water that seemed to have formed a ravine at our gate. After we levelled half of it out, we put down 26 tonnes of gravel and rotavated the other side with good, nutritious soil, and prepared the ground to create a new lawn.

When all the preparation was done, the soil levelled off and rolled down firmly, we sowed the grass seeds. It was surprisingly hot when we did this, a rare couple of weeks of baking English sunshine and not a single drop of rain. Dad warned me sternly, as he was putting his tools in his van getting ready to leave, that I needed to go out there and water it with the hose every day. After a week of obeying his instruction, watering and checking it closely, I saw no sign of grass. Then still no growth after two weeks. After that, I called Mum and she handed the phone over to Dad, asking him, half-jokingly, 'What's going on with this grass?'

Dad said, 'Be patient. It will come.'

Each day after that, I kept watering and checking, even lying down on the ground and looking as closely as possible at the seed. But still nothing, not a single bit of green.

I phoned Dad again a little frustrated and said, 'Is there something wrong with that seed? There's still no grass coming through.'

Dad was calm and didn't seem worried at all, which annoyed me more. 'It will come. Don't worry,' he reassured me.

Truth be told, I gave up on it; but lo and behold, within a couple of weeks there appeared a thin layer of grass all across the patch. After a month, some areas became thick, tall grass and Dad said, 'That's where the soil is really fertile.' In other places it was still thin, but nevertheless luscious green right across. I asked Dad, curious and a little embarrassed, reflecting on my impatient doubts, why it had taken so much longer to germinate than the grass we had sown in the front garden.

Dad simply said, 'Sometimes it does.'

I found that's just the way Dad thinks. He has a patient anticipation, a vision about how things could look in the future. He pruned the pear trees in the front garden in the winter so they could grow better fruit for the summer. He cut the unkempt roses hidden at the back of the garden so the flowers they produced the following year would be more beautiful, ones we could cut and take inside the house to enjoy. He thought about the shade that bushes would offer years down the line, and planted the appropriate shrubs around them in response. He knows growth will inevitably happen if the right elements are present. Water, sun and some nutrition. If he plants a tree or sows a seed, he doesn't spend any time questioning whether things will grow; he has total belief they will. Dad, like all good gardeners, is focused on envisioning the best place for things to develop and how to make a garden beautiful for many generations to enjoy.

## Sowers reap

I'm not naturally patient. Maria reminds me of that a lot. Working with Dad in the garden made me realise it would benefit me greatly if in my pursuit of God I started seeing myself like a gardener. Dad believes, like the apostle Paul, that 'a man reaps what he sows' (Galatians 6:7). You may have felt before that your pursuit of God is pointless. I have heard people say things like 'I feel nothing', 'It doesn't seem to go in' or 'I just feel like I'm wasting my time'. It reminds me of when I anxiously complained to Dad on the phone, staring out of my window at the soil that was supposed to be a lawn. A useful key has been adopting the psyche of a gardener.

## Our instant world

Let me explain more. As I've previously addressed, it's no wonder we give up when we measure our time with God based on how we feel afterwards. We are living in the information age, every day bombarded by a tidal wave of information. We have access to people's life and work at the click of a button. I can learn how to change the filter on my washing machine, do my tax forms or start a business just by watching a few videos on YouTube. We don't want to wait any more. Everything is expected to be fast; you can order almost anything and get it delivered to your house within a day. I caught myself getting frustrated with my phone the other day because a video I was watching buffered for about three or four seconds. We are all conditioned to believe that things should happen quickly. It feels very tempting to give up if something doesn't seem to benefit us immediately. But we must not get sucked into the world's narrative which says 'Produce now' and demands nothing less than immediate visible return. We need to see ourselves like gardeners who are blessed with heavenly vision, confident that if they sow, it's impossible in God's timing to not see growth. As gardeners faithfully push seeds into the soil, they imagine plants that will stand tall and beautiful, and so we also must confidently sow spiritual seeds that will eventually produce a great harvest.

> Do not be deceived: God cannot be mocked. A man reaps what he sows. Whoever sows to please their flesh, from the flesh will reap destruction; whoever sows to please the Spirit, from the Spirit will reap eternal life. Let us not become weary in doing good, for at the proper time we will reap a harvest if we do not give up.
>
> (Galatians 6:7–9)

If I keep intentionally dedicating time, and fall in love with sowing in the Spirit where no one sees, where it's not always fireworks and euphoria, I will see astonishing, lasting fruit pop up in my life, and then again in my children's lives and their children's lives. That's why sowing today matters; we are investing. Sometimes it will bring you to tears and you will feel a tangible delight well up in your heart as you, in real time, witness germination happening in your heart. But at other times, it will feel insignificant and your mind will wander to places far away from God. But if we keep sowing into our pursuit of God, no matter what, growth is inevitable; roots will push in deeper than yesterday and branches will slowly extend, holding great fruit.

My dad has a quiet confidence about him. He's very patient and understated, but he lights up when he talks about stuff that often bores people, such as soil types and different breeds of sheep. He has a calm way about him. That's the only way I can describe it, almost as if he has learnt up close from creation itself that life is innate and change can't be forced. Making things grow is a creator's job. I think Dad knows that more than many.

## Mountainside secrets

### TIP 9
Faithfully sow with time into your pursuit of God and leave the
fruit to him.

## PRAYER FOR THOSE FAITHFULLY SOWING

O God, give me the faith of an old gardener who has sown patiently and seen the way you make things grow. Give me eyes to perceive the abundant harvest I'm going to reap. You are not a cheap get-rich-quick scheme to me. Silence and expose the foe and thief who whispers lies of deceit, condemning my faithful sowing with pressure to compete. Lord, I believe that if I sow, I will surely reap.

# 18

# BODYBUILDING MENTALITY

*Now, as you begin to move into Him, He will gradually take possession of your heart. He gains it the same way – little by little ... if God is your mover, you will go much farther in a short time than all your repeated self effort could ever do.*

JEANNE GUYON

I've had a gym membership a couple of times in my life but it never lasted long. I'm naturally a thin build and I struggle to put on weight. I could eat any amount of food and it would never show on my waistline. Maria tells me that I don't know how lucky I am.

The gym is a strange place though. I remember, when I was 16 and I first joined one, feeling incredibly awkward about my thin arms, standing sheepishly watching men with bigger biceps than my thighs slamming weights to the floor. It was intimidating to say the least. I didn't know all the gym etiquette, so I stumbled around self-consciously from machine to machine, apologising to people after interrupting their sets. I joined mainly because all my friends had; I had no expectation of being an Arnold Schwarzenegger. *I just don't have the build for it*, I would constantly remind myself, probably to further tame my expectations.

But after a surprising week of joining and a few enthusiastic sessions, I actually thought something was happening. I tensed my muscles at home in the mirror, feeling confidence bubble up in me. I told myself that I was looking big. I started thinking it was possible, that even though I'm a thin build I might actually get a big chest and some impressive biceps. I started looking around at people more in the gym and thinking to myself, *Not long and you'll look something like that.*

Another thing I discovered at the gym was physiology. I must have not been concentrating when we learned about it at school. I found out really quickly we have an incredible amount of muscles in our body. I left sessions hardly being able to walk. I remember thinking as I pressed down with my fingers on aching muscles, *I didn't even know you existed!*

In the previous chapter I presented the benefits of seeing ourselves like gardeners, who faithfully sow with a great harvest in mind. I also think we should view ourselves like bodybuilders. Maybe bodybuilding gardeners. Developing a secret place with God is similar to developing biceps or defined abs.

I found out that bodybuilders know two things that are very helpful to us in our pursuit of God.

**1. They are in it for the long haul.** After a couple of months of going to the gym, I realised it was the same people I saw again and again. I overheard a conversation an older guy with big wrinkly muscles was having. He was telling a much younger guy in his twenties across the room how he'd been working out since he was a teenager. Building muscles takes time; I know that now, but I don't think I did when I first joined the gym. I went with an expectation of quick results: after a few weeks of going I was positive I would be filling out all my T-shirts. Similar to gardeners, to see any significant long-term growth you have to decide to be in it for the long haul. And honestly, the same applies to our spirituality.

**2. Be wise about the weight you are able to lift.** If you join the gym and do really long sessions, lifting heavier weights than you can handle, trying to meet ridiculously high goals, the chances are you will become frustrated, or worse, get injured. I've quit the gym three times and ended up paying for my membership without going for months until my contract has expired. That hurts even more than the achy muscles. It's crucial in this journey, whatever point you are at, that you continue to acknowledge that you are building new muscles that need time to develop. Bodybuilders are masters in knowing how much weight to use. Too much can damage and discourage you; too little will not cause any growth at all.

## Habits

In the gym, people are always tensing their muscles in the mirror and staring around comparing themselves with other people. I find I can do the same thing with my time with God. I've heard people say, 'I had such an amazing time with God this morning,' and sometimes I would silently question, *What's wrong with me? Why do I still find it hard to sit still for ten minutes?* One thing that has really set me free is understanding that for every person *muscles take time to grow*. In fact scientists say it takes on average 66 days to develop a new habit.

I learned a lot about habits from reading Charles Duhigg's book *The Power of Habit*. Interestingly, he says:

> If you try to scare people into following Christ's example, it's not going to work for too long. The only way you get people to take responsibility for their spiritual maturity is to teach them habits of faith. Once that happens, they become self-feeders. People follow Christ not because you've led them there, but because it's who they are.

If growth happens over time, not in quick bursts, then we need to create habits that help us commit long term. Our lives are made up of different habits. After a while, we will not consider them habits or practices but a joyful part of our connection with Jesus.

## Celebration is the secret sauce

Celebration is not only a biblical principle, but is also proven by psychologists to be like fertiliser to new habits. B. J. Fogg, who is the founder and director of the Behavior Design Lab at Stanford University, suggests that from the research he has done many people have found many ways to tell themselves that they did a bad job, but few ways of saying they did a good job. I agree; if we want to strengthen the roots of new habits, we must learn to celebrate small victories. This is not a trivial thing. When you recognise that this is a lifelong mission, not just to get ripped for a summer regime, you can celebrate small steps of progress. Don't wait till you're lifting tyres above your head to celebrate your progress. We have to keep reminding ourselves: 'I am building new muscles.' Celebrate yourself. It's the bodybuilders' secret sauce.

We need the psyche of a gardener who sees a beautiful garden before it exists, pulling meaning into our mundane decisions, drawing us with a joyful confidence to keep sowing no matter the weather. But also we need the mentality of a bodybuilder, who understands the way new muscles are effectively built.

Take a moment to respond to these two thoughts:
1. What progress can I celebrate today in my pursuit of God?
   *Write whatever comes to mind, big or small!*
2. In Chapter 16 we identified a time and place we would commit to being with Jesus. We now need to consider the length of time we should commit to this. *Remember, bodybuilders put enough weight on the bar to challenge them to grow but not too much that they*

*will become disheartened and overwhelmed. Pick a length of time that will do this for you!*

_____

_____

_____

◇◇◇◇◇◇◇◇◇◇◇◇◇

*Mountainside secrets*

### TIP 10
Think like a bodybuilder as you celebrate your spiritual muscles growing.

## PRAYER FOR THOSE BUILDING NEW SPIRITUAL MUSCLES

Lord, I repent for staring around the gym and comparing my muscles with others'. I'm sorry for putting unrealistic expectations on myself. Today I'm leaving that way behind. I want more than anything to be a joyful, faithful sower who delights in the process of sowing. I celebrate the fact that I even read this chapter and started this journey – what a victory that was! I'm in this for the long haul, not a short sprint. I want to build muscles, not ones for show but ones that give me strength to live for you. Father, thank you that you are not rushing me on like many others but that you love me right now, not a future more muscular version of me.

# 19

# FINAL WORDS

The more I grow as a leader and carry more weight and responsibility, the more deeply I'm afraid that's all I'll be. A good leader. I'm petrified I'll have good communication skills or respect from a group of people and that will be enough. Because lately I've felt it again, amongst it all – a quiet rumble in my depths convincing me that *being in love with God* is the bullseye. That's what is worth living and dying for like nothing else.

Brennan Manning says:

> Leadership in the church is not entrusted to successful fund-raisers, brilliant biblical scholars, administrative geniuses, or spellbinding preachers ... but to those who have been laid

waste by a consuming passion for Christ – passionate men and women for whom privilege and power are trivial compared to knowing and loving Jesus.

There are 613 commandments in the Jewish law. That's a lot of rules. The Pharisees challenge Jesus in Matthew 22 in hopes of tripping him up. 'What's the greatest command of them all?' they probe. Jesus shows no signs of hesitation. He replies confidently, 'Love the Lord your God with all your heart and with all your soul and with all your mind.' Simple as that.

Out of all the laws, this is the one at the top of the pile, the one with the most weight. Love God. Dr Brian Simmons, who created The Passion Translation, translates this scripture: 'Love the Lord your God with every passion of your heart.'

From the poet King David who writes 'Passion for God's house has consumed me' (Psalm 69:9 NLT) to the *Passion of Christ* movie written and directed by Mel Gibson, it's clear that passion is synonymous with following the way of Jesus.

Thomas Moore, in his book *Care of the Soul*, says that passion simply means 'to be affected' by something. To love God passionately is to have been affected by him.

It's clear the disciples had been affected by Jesus because even the people who fiercely opposed them saw it. 'These men have been with Jesus!' they exclaimed (see Acts 4:13).

## FINAL WORDS

If we are with him in the way I've tried to convey in this book it will surely not be long before we become affected by him and our hearts fill with passion. Then we will shout 'Amen!' as we utter Brennan's words as our own and seek to be completely laid waste by this consuming passion, making it the defining principle of our lives.

*\*\*\**

Life moves on, relationships change, jobs and focuses get redirected. The house Maria and I worked on for so long got sold and we moved into a small flat in the centre of Bath. Maria has a new job in a law firm; I'm doing lots with young people in our city. Life keeps happening, that's for sure. You don't have to live long to realise that our human experience is marked by a *Hobbit*-like journey, with many victories and raised glasses but also devastating defeats that seem to steal all our words. The fact is, our external worlds are unpredictable. The last little while, things haven't been going the way I thought they would. I've faced disappointments. Not huge ones – in fact some of them might seem trivial to you – but lots of small ones have collected like a handful of splinters. Friends are struggling, people I love have died, and I'm trying to be a good leader whilst feeling everyone's post-pandemic fatigue.

I wrote this in my journal one morning in a very honest moment whilst expressing how I felt. It gives you a snapshot of where I was at:

I feel disappointed with my lack of devotion. I feel lacking in joy and happiness. I feel apathetic, needy and thirsty for pleasure. I'm tired of following up with people, tired of being let down. I want to be free of people's opinions. I want to be connected to God and myself. I feel anxious, in my head and all over the place …

Shortly after this, feeling restless, I decided to go on one of my slow wrestling walks by the canal and made a discovery. I could see clearly how I'd been fighting with it all. Throwing fists at what was happening and not happening around me and consequently getting wearied by the battling. But on that walk by the canal as I wrestled, I started to see with clarity that the greatest chaos was stemming from within. Whilst I was distracted by all the challenges being presented by life, I had neglected that which I knew mattered most. It was as if in the quiet of the familiar canal God poked his head up and said 'Hey'.

I have found and continually rediscover that the internal life, the place where our essence seeks to commune with God's essence, is where true peace flows from. That place can stay nourished and healthy at all times. It's an interesting thing to feel fragility all around you, yet also be internally anchored. It's hard to describe. But that's how I started to feel by the canal. Weakened and tired, yet full of strength. Ultimately on that walk I was reawakened again to the truth – that the further I divert from a constant, secret, daily pursuit of God, the more I begin to fall apart inside. And falling apart inside is the worst type of falling apart.

That was the loss of it all. Yes, there were some real, painful and tangible losses at that time, but what hurt the most is I had chosen to abandon my normal rhythm. I had abandoned my pursuit of God and settled for all the cheap ways of measuring yourself.

A neglected and broken-down private pursuit of God causes us to become victims of whatever is happening around us. But when we keep finding Jesus and our hearts become personally affected by him, we are internally energised even when life is unfolding around us.

Honestly I felt silly by the canal that day. Annoyed I had missed it again after learning the lesson repeatedly. I realised again, soberly, that no one has God-privileges. Who am I to think I will grow in intimacy with God just because I have good intentions or past achievements? The way to Jesus is set, and a feast awaits every son and daughter who bravely leaves the crowd to take a seat at the table.

Thank you for reading all the way to the end of this short book. I pray the words would lead you again and again to the table to feast, to be affected by Jesus in a way that slowly changes everything within you.

## Final prayer
Jesus, here I am again.
Take my life and teach me to find you.

## MOUNTAINSIDE SECRETS

Convince me, even more deeply, that knowing and being known by you is the most significant gift I'll ever discover. I want to be laid waste by a consuming passion for Christ. Give me courage to leave the crowd and climb the mountain.

# ACKNOWLEDGEMENTS

It feels very surreal that I'm releasing this book. It's been a joyful yet incredibly challenging task. I feel extremely grateful and slightly surprised to be at the stage of the process where I get to write these thanks. I consider myself extremely privileged to have been surrounded by people who have lived this message for decades and have greatly influenced me in becoming who I am today.

Bob Sorge you are one of those people, I'm so grateful for the-forward you have written but more importantly this message that you live. This book was greatly inspired by your own work, so thank you.

Thank you to my family; Jenny, Geof, James, Steve and Hannah you have provided many stories in this book and you each embody so much of who I want to become.

Jon and Ruth and the whole Life Church family in Bath, thankyou. This community is the soil that much of my growing has taken place and where this initial hunger for knowledge of God was discovered. Special thank you to Found Youth, the wonderful young people who tease me so often but keep reminding me that this life following Jesus is not that complicated. Eleanor, Anna, Sophie, Sofia, Judah, Olivia and Jonny thank you for joining me on zoom at 8am in 2020 when the pandemic hit, daring yourselves to develop a private pursuit of God. Those conversations sparked the idea for this book.

Josh Smith, words can't express my gratitude for all you have poured into these words. Thank you for teaching me years ago our best work here on earth happens within the heart. You have given me so much confidence whilst writing and continually sought to elevate my words like they are your own.

I'm honoured to be releasing this book with Orphan No More, a community of friends convinced of the redemptive power of Art. For many years the whole Orphan No More community has been a source of encouragement, which has kept me creating and believing in the power of words.

Thank you Hanna Glover, Mary King, Ellis Naylor, Mandy and Grant Shipley and many others for reading early material

## ACKNOWLEDGEMENTS

and carefully helping refine these words. Likewise Paul and Zaccmedia you have been absolutely incredible to work with in the editing process, I'm blown away by how you have turned these words into a real book.

Most of all I want to thank my gorgeous wife Maria. You are simply the greatest. Thanks for your strength mingled with tenderness and for giving me space and time to write this book. I know it's been a cost. Thanks for reading and re reading countless edits; late at night, on planes and holidays. More importantly, thanks for continually giving me courage to keep going. I honestly couldn't have done it without you.

# POSTSCRIPT

## Mountainside secrets

**HIS SECRET CHAPTER**
TIP 1: Being with Jesus must involve being alone with him.

**CASH-MACHINE CHRISTIANITY**
TIP 2: The fruit of being with Jesus is who you are slowly becoming.

**LEAVE YOUR CAMERA IN THE CAR**
TIP 3: A great way to be with Jesus is to learn to behold him.

**LEARNING TO LIVE DETHRONED**
TIP 4: Approach God's presence through wholehearted surrender.

**WRESTLING WITH GOD**
TIP 5: We can approach God through surrender by wrestling.

**DISARMED**
TIP 6: Practise surrender by the way of stillness.

OPENINGS EVERYWHERE
TIP 7: Approach God with the mentality that there is always an open door to his presence.

WHEN AND WHERE
TIP 8: Decide when and where you will be alone with Jesus.

PSYCHE OF A GARDENER
TIP 9: Faithfully sow with time into your pursuit of God and leave the fruit to him.

BODYBUILDING MENTALITY
TIP 10: Think like a bodybuilder as you celebrate your spiritual muscles growing.

# ABOUT THE AUTHOR

Pastor and poet Timothy is passionate about seeing people become captivated by the beauty and wonder of knowing God. Based in Bath, Timothy is married to Maria and together they belong to the Life Church community where they are part of the leadership team, overseeing youth and a Sunday evening gathering called "The Well'. Timothy has released a number of spoken word EP's as well as being a part of the Orphan No More collective. Timothy is proud to be launching his first book this year called "Mountainside Secrets".

Printed in Great Britain
by Amazon